LIVING UN pLUggED

Young Adults,
Faith and
The UncOmmOn Life

PAM PETERS-PRIES

F&L
FAITH & LIFE
PRESS

Newton, Kansas
Winnipeg, Manitoba

Printed in the United States of America.

International Standard Book Number 0-87303-251-9
Library of Congress Number 95-83909

Editorial direction by Susan E. Janzen; copyediting by Mary L. Gaeddert;
design by Ron Tinsley; desktop formatting by Ilene Franz; printing by
Mennonite Press, Inc.

CONTENTS

**To Grandma and Grandpa Peters,
my mentors and friends**

1. Unplug!

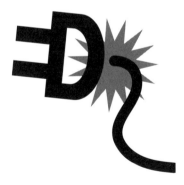

A growing number of artists in the music industry are turning to acoustic instruments and less technical recording processes to make "unplugged" recordings—recordings with a more "natural" sound. For many musicians and music fans, this trend has provided a refreshing alternative to the high-tech, highly engineered, "electronic" sound of many current recordings.

"Unplugged" recordings have their counterparts in many other aspects of life. Health-food stores offer "natural, wholesome" alternatives to highly processed and packaged foods. Herbal or homeopathic treatments offer an alternative to the synthetic drugs and high-tech equipment of mainstream medicine. Stores and catalogues offer clothing and linen made from organically grown fibres processed "naturally." Handmade items are popular alternatives to those mass produced in factories.

But don't let this deluge of unplugged recordings and other low-tech trends delude you into thinking that the high-tech era is fading into oblivion. The processed, packaged, engineered, and electronic in our society still rule the day. High-tech and low-tech continue to co-exist in our world—symbols of the recent explosion of information and options that underscore our need to both continually expand our horizons and keep things at a simple, understandable level. If anything, the rise in popularity of low-tech alternatives may only complicate life in a world already teeming with ideas and alternatives. With so much information and so many choices to sort through already, does anyone really need more?

This is your life

You grew up in a world of rapid change, complex issues, and increasing anxiety. The conflict between high-tech and low-tech is only one of the many conflicts, choices, and issues you face daily. Environmental disaster. Economic collapse. Family disintegration. Moral erosion. Educational failure. Potential personal and global catastrophe constantly lie in wait. This is your life—at least in part.

Many glimmers of hope beckon in the landscape of your life and world, and many very positive things are taking place around you. Yet the last twenty years have seen unprecedented change that leaves many people feeling overwhelmed, if not completely incapacitated. What are the things that have shaped your life and the lives of those around you?

Rapidly increasing options. You have more options than any previous generation in history. Exchange programs, the possibility of employment in multinational corporations with offices all over the world, and the ease of global travel have increased your opportunities to visit and live in various communities around the world to levels that your forebears would never have dreamed possible. Rapidly changing technology continuously creates new jobs. The disintegration of traditional gender roles allows for more choice at home and at work for men and women. Ever-widening definitions of the nuclear family are creating new freedom and possibilities for structuring your home life.

Options create freedom, and that freedom can be a significant driving force in your life. However, increasing options also increase the need for decision making, creating an increase in anxiety. Thus, this option explosion creates stress that can become overwhelming.

Decreasing options. Paradoxically, your world is also one of fewer options. This is most noticeable in the areas of education and work, where increasing competition for a decreasing number of positions can significantly narrow your options for possible training or employment. Technology creates many new job opportunities but makes other jobs obsolete. Multinational corporations look abroad for international opportunities yet lay off people in North America. The general downward mobility predicted for your generation may reduce your options due to more limited financial means.

Individualism. You live in a world that believes that right and wrong are matters of personal opinion. On the one hand, this can create a tremendous sense of

personal freedom. On the other hand, it can create significant difficulties as diverse people with diverse
opinions live together in the same world. This trend
toward individualism can also create confusion as you
reflect on your Christian faith. How do you maintain
belief in the existence and lordship of God while living
in a world that likes to do its own thing?

Catastrophe. You've grown up with a perpetual
sense of potential catastrophe. Thanks to recently
established and rapidly expanding global electronic
media linkups, you have the potential to see a lot, hear
a lot, and know a lot.

Our media doesn't have the time to present all the
information available. So they pick out the interesting,
the unusual, the noteworthy. Though 450 jets carrying
50,000 passengers may have landed safely today, we'll
hear about the one that crashed, killing all 125 people
on board. Is it any wonder that a lot of young adults
get a skewed, anxiety-producing picture of the world?
None of us want to live in the evening news.

The rise of the special-interest group. Special-interest
groups—lobbying groups representing increasingly
smaller sectors of the population—have enjoyed
tremendous growth in recent years. Riding on a wave
of political correctness and concern for the environment and marginalized people, we are subjected almost
daily to news of yet another group that has somehow
been oppressed, suppressed, or otherwise marginalized.
The cries of these groups usually include pleas for our

money, time, or prayer in support of their causes. The persistent and poignant voices of special-interest groups add to the already overwhelming picture of the world in which you are living.

Charting the uncharted territory

Increasing options. Decreasing options. Individualism. Potential catastrophe. Special-interest groups. You are subjected to an incredible number of options, ideas, issues, and concerns. Is it any wonder that anxiety and delayed adulthood (that is, the avoidance of choice and responsibility) are words often used to characterize your generation? Where can you go to learn the skills you need to cope adequately with your life and world?

Being more reactive than proactive, our society doesn't quite know what to do with the information and option explosion it has created. The institutional church, typically even more backward-looking than society, may be less helpful. A good part of the Christian church is still wondering what happened to all those Baby Boomers (your parents)! Few churches are aware enough of all the factors at play in your fast-paced life to help you deal constructively and judiciously with them. Consequently, you may feel more or less on your own to comprehend and cope with a world that somebody else has created for you.

Unplug!

In this book, I encourage you to "unplug." Living

unplugged is living alternatively. It means detaching yourself from the apparatus of our complex world enough to gain some perspective. Unplugging gives you space, time, and a framework from which to evaluate options and information and make effective decisions about your actions and responses. Living unplugged means being tuned in enough to the world to recognize the truly important and meaningful in it. At the same time, living unplugged means maintaining enough distance from the world to avoid being swept up in the current of the truly trivial.

I hope you'll find this book useful in providing for you a screen to sort out the truly important and meaningful from the truly trivial in the information that whizzes past you. I hope you'll find this book helpful in building a framework from which you can evaluate options and information and make effective decisions about your actions and responses. I hope you'll also find this book helpful as a source of encouragement to live faithfully and prophetically in a world that needs a faithful and prophetic voice to cut through the wilderness.

The world is an increasingly diverse, overwhelming, bewildering, and exciting place. Your task is to understand it, thrive in it, change it, and love it. Walk the line between awareness of the world as it is and awareness of creative alternatives. Don't be afraid to live the uncommon life. Unplug!

QUESTIONS FOR DISCUSSION

1. The array of issues you face may not be as over-whelming as I have portrayed here. Individually, make a list of the three issues you feel impact your life to the greatest extent. As a group, brainstorm possible responses to these issues. What changes can you effect as an individual or a group? What changes are beyond your control?

2. I have stated that society and the church work constantly to try to keep up with themselves. Do you agree? Jot down your responses to the following phrases (list more than one response if you feel so moved):

    a. An important issue you feel the church/society is dealing with appropriately is ...

    b. An issue you feel the church/society spends an inappropriate amount of time and energy on is ...

    c. An important issue you wish the church/society would deal with is ...

Do the appropriate responses of the church and society make up for the inappropriate or nonexistent ones? What could you do to assist the church and society in dealing more appropriately with the issues you face? Consider sharing your responses to these questions with leaders in your church or community.

3. Where do you go when you need help making a decision, coping with a problem, or otherwise improving your sense of dealing well with life? Is the church on your resource list? Why or why not?

2. Life Skills 101: Decision Making

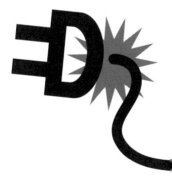

I remember once telling my Mom that I could hardly wait until I was older and my life was more settled. I longed for the day when I would know exactly what I was going to do with the rest of my life, if and to whom I would be married, and exactly how these and other factors would intertwine in the grand scheme of my life. My mother, in the matter-of-fact, sensible, and yet more-unsettling-than-comforting tone she often employs, responded: "Pam, it doesn't get any easier."

She's right. Life doesn't get any easier, at least not in the sense that we can hope to finally reach that moment when past, present, and future life events suddenly come into clear focus and we know—for sure and for-ever—the path our lives will take. Eternal certainty of this nature only comes in books, movies, and occasional moments of extreme optimism or delusion. In real life, there will always be more decisions to make.

What can make life easier, however, is improving your decision-making skills. If you're going to have to make decisions anyway, you might as well make them as painlessly as possible. This is particularly true since the independence and responsibility of adulthood will require more and more decisions of you. The more decisions you have to make, the more you'll want and need a good way of approaching them.

So what is a helpful and relatively painless way to make a decision? There are countless models or techniques you can follow, involving a huge variety of specific steps. All of them boil down to more or less the same thing: When confronted with a situation where a decision is required, list your options, evaluate them, and act on the best one. It sounds pretty simple and straightforward. In real life, making a decision is seldom so neat and precise a process. However, following a few basic guidelines can make the best of some of life's most difficult and messy work.

Name the problem

A decisive action isn't possible until you know what it is you should be decisive about. Accurately naming the issue you are attempting to resolve is an essential first step in any decision-making process.

Begin by naming the feelings that have prompted you to think about making some changes in your life. Uneasiness, anxiety, or dissatisfaction are common ones. Naming feelings is often pretty straightforward. Getting to the source of these feelings may be a more difficult process. Pay attention to the places and times that these feelings are the most notable: at work or school? with your family? with your boyfriend or girlfriend? Your anxiety may surface even when you're just thinking about the situation that's causing it.

Once you have "located" your feelings in this manner (often the biggest job), narrow it down even further. If work makes you anxious, what part of it is causing anxiety? You may find it helpful to list any and all possible causes (e.g., relationships with co-workers, workload, feelings of incompetence, etc.) and let your intuition guide you. The real cause will often "jump off the page" at you, so to speak. If a strained relationship with a co-worker is making you anxious, you need to decide on a specific way of either improving the relationship or terminating it. If a heavy workload is creating anxiety, you need to decide how to reduce it or how to manage your stress better.

Brainstorm

Now you know the issue forcing the decision. What are all the possible ways you could resolve this issue? A decision can only be as good as the options you generate for its resolution, so put some real effort in at this stage. Get out a piece of paper and let the ideas flow unrestrained to your pen. Creativity is essential. If you were functioning with absolutely no constraints— financial, social, personal, or other—what are the possible options you could pursue? Creativity is, after all, essentially shedding the constraints of prevailing patterns of thought. Allowing your thoughts to range this freely may generate some pretty harebrained options, but they're options. There'll be plenty of time to weed out the truly silly stuff later.

Tap the creativity of friends. Don't ask them what they think you should do but what they would do in your situation. You are looking for creative alternatives, not concerned advice. Write down their responses. And remember that brainstorming is best not done in a single sitting. Carry your paper and pen in your pocket for a week. Inspiration may come when you least expect it, and you have better things to do late at night than try to remember the great idea that struck you in the washroom at the mall.

When you feel you couldn't possibly have left a stone unturned, try a second-level brainstorming run. Read your list of options over carefully and thoughtfully. Could some of your harebrained options be pared down or honed to work within the constraints you face? Are there elements of various options that appeal to you and could be combined or rearranged to create other options? Again, write down any new thoughts. Give yourself a well-deserved break, and you're ready to move on to the next stage.

Evaluate your options

There are many different ways of doing this. Some are always helpful. Some make sense only in particular situations. Regardless of the nature of your decision, however, you should employ some method of evaluating your options.

Research. You need to find out enough about every option you are considering to enable you to make choices between them. If you are buying a car, factors like initial cost, fuel efficiency, and reliability will all affect your decision about which particular car to buy. If you are trying to decide whether to join a particular committee at church, find out what your responsibilities would be.

List pros and cons. Thorough research—knowing everything you could possibly know about every option on your list—will never make a decision for you. You are still a factor. You may find a car that is affordable, fuel efficient, and exceptionally reliable, but still be mysteriously drawn to that 1974 Volkswagen camper van that is anything but reliable but seems to have your name written all over it. Knowledge facilitates your decision making, but only in combination with personal preferences and values.

Listing the pros and cons—both objective and subjective—of each option you are considering puts you into the picture. You may even choose to "weight" your pros and cons, giving a 1 to those of least importance to you and a 5 to those of greatest importance. You don't want to make a "decision by number," but going through this exercise may help you to clarify the values and preferences at play in your decision making.

Envision yourself carrying out each of the options. Imagining yourself enacting each possible outcome of your decision helps you tap into feelings about the decision that may not at first be obvious.

Is there an option that makes you feel particularly

satisfied or relieved? Is there one that makes you feel tense or anxious? Your imaginary feelings are likely close to what your actual feelings would be.

You may also wish to discuss your options with a few trusted friends. Invite them to offer their opinion on which option seems the most consistent with you as they know you. This is particularly helpful if you feel you are losing perspective under the weight of your decision.

Don't be afraid to waver. Uncertainty is a self-correcting process. If you are wavering on a decision—if you can't commit yourself wholeheartedly to one particular option—there may be a good reason for your indecision. Somehow, your subconscious may pick up some deeply buried reservations.

Revisit the previous step. Picture yourself carrying out the options you are leaning toward and pay close attention to what you are feeling. Once you have isolated your emotions, think hard about their causes. Are you scared to pursue an option because you think your parents may disapprove? Are you feeling hurried in your decision-making process by the pressures of time or relationships? Repeat this process a few times, perhaps out loud in the presence of good friends, to see if the same reservations emerge consistently. This exercise may leave you with another decision to make (e.g., do you feel strongly enough about your decision to risk your parents' disapproval?), but at least you'll have moved out of paralysis and back into action.

When entering this exercise, however, be ready to face up to your own avoidance. If you've envisioned yourself carrying out your decision several times and find yourself saying, "I know what I need to do; I just need to do it," you are no longer wavering. You are avoiding. Take the plunge. The satisfaction of making a decision will be worth the initial leap of faith it takes to make it.

Take a look at the big picture. You have a developing value system that informs the decisions you make in your life. Use it. Don't ever assume that you can occasionally make even minor decisions that go against your most deeply held beliefs and get away with it. This may be tempting if the decision could potentially bring you some quick, short-term pleasure (a quick decision to have sex is a glaring example), but the long-run consequences may be more than you bargained for. Evaluating your options should always keep in mind who you are and what you believe in at a most basic level.

This is perhaps why generations of wise and sensible folk have counseled against making decisions "in the heat of the moment." Hastily made decisions, particularly about important matters, seldom allow for the self-reflection and analysis necessary to put the decision soundly in the context of your entire life and value system. When the pressure is to act and not think, think twice as hard.

Don't just think about it—do it!

At some point in the decision-making process, you are
going to have to make a decision. This can be scary.
As long as you are simply generating options and evaluating them, you can more or less maintain some level
of detachment in the whole process. It's almost like
being a spectator in your own life.

But the detachment and ease of spectating quickly
vanish when the proverbial rubber will need to hit the
road. Eventually you are going to have to take some
action. The thought of your decision becoming reality
can be paralyzing for a variety of reasons.

Fear of pain. If you know your decision will cause
you some pain or discomfort, fear of that pain is
enough to delay the decision for many of us.
Recognize, however, that avoiding or postponing a
painful decision isn't the same as avoiding pain.
Presumably, you have gone through this whole decision-making process for the purpose of resolving some
situation or issue in your life already causing you pain.
Many decisions to end or resolve such difficult circumstances initially cause more intense pain, which
subsides as we deal with the consequences of the decision. The alternative is to continue to live indefinitely
with the pain of the situation or issue about which you
are deliberating. Reflecting on this alternative may be
enough to eventually move you past your paralysis.

Fear of losing control. When you live in a world
where other people and forces exist, the consequences

of your actions are almost never exactly what you had planned. Some element of the outcome of a decision (e.g., if others will respond the way you think they will) is almost always beyond your control. Is unpredictability reason enough to postpone or avoid a decision you know really needs to be made?

Naturally, there is always a possibility that your decision won't work out exactly as you had planned or hoped. But that's exactly the point—there is always that possibility. You can spend time wondering what exactly would happen if you took a particular course of action, or you can make the decision, discover its consequences, and start dealing with them.

Fear of permanence. The sheer enormity of some decisions can also inhibit our ability to make them. How can you decide today what you are going to do for the rest of your life? How can you decide that twenty or forty years from now you will still be in love with the same person you're in love with right now?

Some decisions are bigger than others, and they should be approached with seriousness. But it's also true that few decisions affect the course of your life to the extent you think they will. This is due to that ever-present factor in the world known as change. People change. Circumstances change. The world changes. People adapt. A decision, even a major one, seldom dictates the course of the rest of your life. It's more accurate to say that it sets a general direction from which you can navigate. Viewing an overwhelming decision as the beginning of a process rather than as the end of a process can help put it into perspective.

Live and learn

I know this isn't all as easy or as straightforward in life as it is on paper. Particularly in young adulthood when such significant issues as future occupation, marital status, and lifestyle need to be dealt with, making decisions can be time-consuming, difficult, and often painful. The process can be further complicated by the fact, as noted in the previous chapter, that you are a member of a generation that faces more options on nearly every front than any previous generation. More options mean more freedom, but also more decisions.

But if the process of making a decision can be a difficult one, the outcome can be very rewarding. Making decisions is the process by which each of us takes control of life and directs its course. Making even a seemingly small or insignificant decision builds confidence, self-esteem, and independence. That's why developing a healthy and effective way to approach decisions is such a necessary life skill. Making good decisions is one of the essential ways we build our autonomy and worth as individuals.

One question still remains: Where does the leading of God come in in all of this? I sometimes envy the certainty enjoyed by many biblical characters. When Joseph wondered whether or not he should divorce Mary, an angel appeared to him in a dream and told him what to do (Matthew 1:19-21). When Gideon doubted God's plan to deliver Israel from the Midianites, he asked for a sign, and got it—not once, but twice (Judges 6:36-40). God's leading has seldom appeared that concretely in my life.

So how can we seek the will of God? On the one hand, the answer is simple—everywhere. Prayer, reflection, Bible study, and discussion with other Christians will be helpful at every step of the decision-making process. And yet the issue is more complex than that. Involving God and inviting God's leading in a particular decision and knowing when and where God is leading are two different things.

I believe that God leads in pretty simple ways, in everyday occurrences that we need to learn to recognize as God's leading. That moment of creativity when a new solution to an old and persistent issue comes to you—that's the leading of God. That nagging sense that what you're about to do might not be the right thing—that's the leading of God. That sense of certainty and satisfaction that you experience when an issue is resolved decisively—that's the leading of God.

It's also important to learn to look at the big picture. Nehemiah's determination to rebuild the walls of Jerusalem was tested at many points—by enemy plots against his plan and by disagreement among his people themselves. And yet, when the wall was finally complete and the Israelites could return to their city, Nehemiah must have known that he had led in doing the work of God. Remembering points in our lives where we have felt confident in God's leading reminds us that God is faithful. God leads us even when we are unaware of it, a promise we need to learn to trust in both the foggy moments and in the crystal clear ones.

QUESTIONS FOR DISCUSSION

1. Do you believe that the number of options your generation has to choose from enhances or jeopardizes your quality of life? Why?

2. Decision making is a skill that requires a lot of practice to master. In pairs or groups of three, take turns sharing situations about which you feel you need to make a decision. Together, work through the process outlined in this chapter up to the moment of actual decision making. After this exercise, ask yourself the following questions. You may choose to discuss them in your small group:

- What parts of the process did you find the most difficult? What can you do to overcome this?
- Where did you find the counsel or insights of others the most helpful? Are you generally ready to or reluctant to accept help from others when making a decision?
- Are you ready to make a decision on this issue? If so, what is it? If not, what is holding you back?

3. Recall a time when you felt certain of God's leading in your life. What was it that gave you such certainty? Have you been able to draw on that certainty in less uncertain times? If so, how? If not, why not?

3. Time Management: Take Control of Your Life Before It Takes Control of You

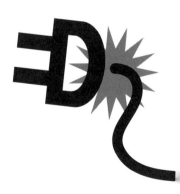

People who know me might laugh at the fact that I have actually written a chapter on time management. I have a widespread reputation as a procrastinator. I am always the first person willing to drop everything and go out for coffee, the only person who actually welcomes interruptions, and the last person to finally start or finish a project, usually in the wee hours of the dreaded night before it's due.

Therefore, I've written this chapter more out of personal struggle than triumph. I've read enough about time management to teach courses on it; I just don't always have the discipline to put my knowledge to work in my life. I offer you the following time-management tips and techniques in the hope that writing them down encourages both you and me to employ them in our lives.

What are we managing, anyway?

The first and foremost thing to remember here is that time management is really self-management (Ted W. Engstrom & R. Alec Mackenzie, *Managing Your Time*, Pyranee Books, 1988, p. 9). We can't really manage the amount of time we have, because time passes at the same rate for all of us. We can only manage the way we use the time that is available.

What's your problem?

Of course, the first step toward better use of your time is to make a fearless, honest assessment of the way you use your time now. Not knowing or not stating accurately what you're currently doing with your time makes it pretty hard to decide what you should be doing differently.

Maybe you are one of those people who always feels like you're trying to do too much. It is difficult to keep up with a full course load, a part-time job, intramural volleyball, church choir, and being a youth sponsor— not to mention the necessities of eating, sleeping, and relaxing. Chronic overcommitment, also known as the inability to say no, is a major time-management problem for a lot of people.

Perhaps your problem is a little different. Rather than feeling that you're doing too much each day, you have a sense of not ever really doing enough. Strangely enough, this problem can easily be mistaken for the previous one, or can go hand-in-hand with it. Making poor use of your time can make even a few responsibilities seem like too many. And if over-committing yourself creates time stress, underusing your time will only magnify it.

Carefully examine your situation

Try keeping a time log for a week or two. Keep a notebook and a watch with you at all times. Take note of what you are doing every minute of the day—and I mean every waking minute. Record the fifteen minutes you spent talking to the friend who didn't get the hint that you were too busy to visit and the ten minutes you spent staring out the window in the middle of that unpleasant task, wishing you didn't have to do it.

At the end of your monitoring period, take stock of the situation. What are your biggest time wasters? Some common ones are interruptions (like the friend you couldn't get rid of), procrastination (pursuing trivial tasks as a delusion of productivity while avoiding the things that really need to be done), and lack of concentration (staring out windows, biting nails, and jumping from task to task without completing any of them). Where is most of your productive time spent— on work or study? volunteer activities? household maintenance? Are these time allocations in keeping with your personal values and the demands of necessity or reality?

Now that you have a fairly realistic picture of where your time goes, some light should be appearing at the end of the time-management tunnel. As they say, identifying or admitting to a problem is the first step toward solving it. If you take advantage of the time-management tips in this chapter, you may find that there are enough hours in the day (and then some) for all of your commitments.

The one big problem
Of course, it is possible that you're already managing

your time perfectly well, but that would make you a rare exception, according to time-management experts. The pervasiveness of poor time management reported by these folks implies that good time management is basically contrary to human nature—an idea with which I am inclined to agree.

I say this because of one great underlying problem that plagues many of us, rendering us more or less unable to use our time well—lack of self-discipline. We don't have the self-discipline to concentrate for extended periods of time, to say no to an additional task, to meet self-imposed deadlines or goals, to tackle an unpleasant task. You get the picture.

If you, like most of the rest of us, are low on self-discipline, it's easy to fall into a pit of despair over time management. It's one thing to identify your time-management problems and learn about possible solutions. It is an entirely different manner to muster up the self-discipline required to put these solutions to work. At this stage of the game, many of us just plain give up.

But there is hope. Just as so many time-management problems are interrelated (i.e., related to self-discipline problems), so are their solutions. If you are able to overcome your lack of self-discipline in one area, the behavior will spill over into other areas. As you read over the time-management tips yet to come, try not to be overwhelmed by the magnitude of the task before you. Choose one very small, very specific way to begin your attempt to overcome your time-management problems. Enlist any minute particle of self-discipline you do possess to pursue this tiny undertaking. When this very small, specific behaviour becomes a good habit, undertake to learn another. You will find the rewards of this process often outweigh the effort required to keep it in motion, making it a very self-reinforcing action. So take heart. The self-discipline required for good time management can be learned.

What are you going to do about it?

Thus far, you've identified what your particular time-management problem is and convinced yourself it is possible to overcome it. Now it's time to explore some solutions. Oddly enough, the remedies for poor time management seem to be more or less the same regardless of its causes. A few basic suggestions and we should be on the way to becoming productive, satisfied, and relaxed people.

Set goals. Goal-setting is a dominant theme in all of the time-management literature. The basic idea here is that an organized and well-directed person fares better in life than a disorganized or misdirected person—which should come as no surprise to us. We can let our lives and tasks unfold haphazardly in relation to the time we have and hope that some fortunate coincidences take place. Or we can plan ahead of time to have the right tasks take place at the right time. Goal-setting, which begins with long-range vision, gives us a sense of where we are headed, a necessary prerequisite for planning the best way to get there.

So ask yourself where you would like to be, or where others are requiring you to be, several weeks, months, or even years down the road. Once you've identified your long-term goal or goals, work backwards, establishing short-term goals. Maybe you want to have all your term papers written two weeks before the end of the term so you'll have time to do some Christmas shopping. Your short-term goals would probably be self-imposed deadlines by which you'd like to have each individual paper finished. From short-term goals, work back to daily "to do" lists—listing specific tasks you will accomplish each day to make your goals a reality. Sound easy? Reading about it is probably easier than doing it, but it's certainly a good place to start.

Be realistic. For me, the easiest part of time management is making "to do" lists. Keeping them, of course, is an entirely different matter. I get overzealous and write down absolutely every task that I might possibly be able to get done today. I tend to hope that seeing the tremendous amount of things that need doing will frighten me into getting at it and convince me that today is the day that I need to begin using my time properly.

Time-management experts, however, recommend the use of positive rather than negative reinforcement. Therefore, helpful counsel is to be as realistic as possible in creating your "to do" lists and your goals, whether they are for today, this week, or the next decade. You are aiming for that self-satisfied, glorious feeling that comes from crossing off the items on your list, until by the end of the allotted time period, they're all done. Reveling in the tremendous satisfaction of getting everything done, perhaps even with a bit of time to spare, increases your resolve to use your time as well again the next day.

If it should happen that you don't accomplish everything on your list, relax and ask yourself what happened. Were you unrealistic about the number of tasks you could accomplish or the length of time it would take for certain ones? Did you encounter unexpected and unavoidable interruptions or complications? Or did you simply waste too much time? This exercise points us to one of the basic lessons of time management and life in general: use mistakes or downfalls as opportunities for learning rather than self-flagellation. Today's tragedies can become tomorrow's triumphs.

Be specific. Remember, you're aiming for positive reinforcement. You want to know when a task is done so you can put that stroke through it on your list. Avoid making lists consisting of vague tasks like "Do homework" or "Plan volunteer-appreciation dinner." Break larger tasks up into smaller, more specific ones. For example, "Plan volunteer-appreciation dinner" could be broken down into "Book banquet hall," "Choose menu," and "Send invitations."

Being specific is particularly helpful when a task seems to have no end. Take, for example, studying for a biology exam. Technically, you're never finished studying—you just run out of time. By listing specific things that you can do to study for biology, you can reassure yourself that you are getting something done, and so making good use of your time. Try "Memorize key terms in Chapter 5," "Review polysaccharide structure," and "Do self-test at end of Chapter 5."

Plan your tasks for the right time of day. Try to plan your day to use your most productive times for the most important tasks. If you experience the typical post-lunch sleepy time most of us do, don't choose that time to do the final edit on your major term paper or annual report. Try washing your coffee cup or returning your library books instead. Contrary to popular student wisdom, this also means that the middle of the night isn't the best time to be doing anything other than sleeping.

Of course, there are situations where this tip will be beyond your control to implement. Most of us relate to some "higher-ups" who make at least some of our decisions about when we do what. School administrators, for example, continue to schedule 1 o'clock classes despite generations of bleary-eyed instructors and students struggling to stay awake through them. But to the extent that you are able to control your own scheduling, make use of this tip. Not only will you make the best use of your time—you'll do it in the area where it counts the most.

Do the worst task first. Like I said earlier, good time-management skills and basic human nature seem to be somewhat contrary phenomena. I don't know anybody who would naturally start their day with the most unpleasant task they had to do. Obviously, implementing this tip requires more than a little self-discipline. Resist the temptation to leave the yucky stuff till "later." You'll enjoy your day a lot more knowing the worst is behind you than dreading that it's yet to come.

By doing this, you'll also avoid the extremely unpleasant situation of having absolutely no choice but to finally tackle that awful task when the deadline is breathing down your neck. I say extremely unpleasant not only because you'll be panicking about whether you'll get the job done at all, let alone done well, but also because things are always twice as awful just because you have absolutely no choice about them.

Concentrate on one task until it's finished. This sounds a lot like just plain common sense, but it's more difficult and less commonly done than most of us would think. How many times have you read the same page over six times without really reading it because you were thinking about all the other things you needed to do? or been caught having completely forgotten who you're phoning by the time the person answers because you're preoccupied with the letter you're trying to write at the same time?

Getting sidetracked is particularly easy when you're worried about forgetting something or when you have several tasks that you're afraid won't be done on time. If, in the middle of a task, you remember something else that needs to be done, jot it down on your "to do" list. Then you can be confident you won't forget about it and can carry on with the task at hand. If there are several pressing items on your plate, you have a better chance of getting at least some of them done if you concentrate on one item at a time. By doing so, you avoid the time wasted by constantly reorienting yourself when you jump from one job to the next, or by worrying that none of the jobs will get finished.

Be positive. Remember that it is possible to learn good time-management skills. We manage to learn all sorts of behaviors that are contrary to human nature—like working eight-hour days and actually enjoying a cup of coffee. Why shouldn't our unnatural behaviors extend to managing our time? With a little bit of patience, perseverance, positive thinking, and self-discipline, these time-management techniques will become nothing more than good habits—like remembering to floss and looking both ways before you cross the street. And you'll be a better person for it (how's that for a cliche?)!

Take control of your life before it takes control of you

It seems to me that people in our society, especially young people, are getting busier and busier and more and more stressed all the time. This is due in large part to ever-increasing societal pressures to be wealthy, respected, "successful" people. Lots of us are bending over backwards to make sure we'll get the right job where we'll earn the right amount of money to enable us to buy the right things. We end up overcommitted, overstressed, and under-satisfied.

Life isn't only about success in society's eyes. If good time management becomes a tool you use to work more so you can earn more so you can spend more, I hope you never master it. Good time management, I believe, is ultimately about achieving a more balanced, spiritual life. It should be about structuring our days so that there is time to just hang out and think about, talk about, or do the things that make our lives meaningful—pursue relationships, explore our faith, enjoy art, engage in social action—that kind of stuff.

Sound a little hippyish? Maybe so, but does that mean it's bad? You'll likely need to do something with some part of your life that will enable you to pay a few bills and buy a few necessary things, but don't let it become all-consuming. Work can be very satisfying, but not if it's all you do. Buck the trend. Take the time to create a balanced life. I think you will find your-selves a lot richer for it.

QUESTIONS FOR DISCUSSION

1. Time for a fearless and honest assessment! Keep a time log for at least a week and consider sharing it with other members of the group. What are your time-management pitfalls? What tips in this chapter could you employ to overcome these pitfalls?

2. What do you think about the necessity of leading a balanced life? Is it actually a necessity or just a luxury? How balanced do you feel your life is? What changes could you make to come closer to the balance you desire?

4. Career Choices: The Good, the Bad, and the Ugly

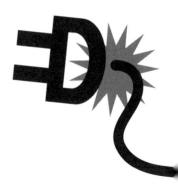

L ike it or not, our North American culture counts what we do for a living as a large part of our identity. This is clear even in the ways questions about one's occupation are phrased. When you were a child, people asked, "What do you want to be when you grow up?" And now that you're older and presumably making more decisions about "what you want to be," people ask simply, "What do you do?" implying that what you are studying or what you do for a living somehow defines your identity.

Our responses often reinforce rather than challenge the assumption that occupation equals identity. Let's say you have taken a job as a gas station attendant with the intention of making some money in order to go back to school. If someone asks you what you do, you will likely say you are a gas station attendant, but with a disclaimer like "just for now" or "just to earn some money for school." You want to make clear to this person that it is just a job for you—it's not something you are or want to be.

Decisions about what you will do for a living are some of the most anxiety-producing decisions you will make. We all want to have occupations that will be rewarding financially, satisfying personally, and valued by society—a tall order, to say the least. Is there a decision that could possibly satisfy all those criteria? Or should you be examining the criteria themselves? And where should you start in this overwhelming affair?

Start with a good look at yourself

The financial rewards and status in society of certain occupations are somewhat beyond your ability to control. Personal satisfaction, on the other hand, is within your reach. You are the person who's going to have to do the work you choose. If you want to be satisfied in your work, take your interests and abilities into careful consideration.

It's a good idea to sit down with a pen and piece of paper and make some lists. Start with a list of the things you are good at doing:

- In what areas have you excelled or do you excel academically? (e.g., maths, sciences, humanities, languages, etc.)
- What are your nonacademic skills? (e.g., social skills, organizational skills, etc.)
- Do you work well in a group setting, or do you prefer to do things alone?
- Do you need a structured environment to function well, or do you thrive when you're able to go about tasks more freely?
- Are you good at meeting deadlines, or do you tend to procrastinate?

All of these factors will have significant bearing on choosing an occupation that is suited to you.

Once you have a list of things that you're good at, take time to make a list of things you really enjoy. These two lists may look similar, since most of us tend to enjoy things we're good at and to dislike things we find difficult, but there may be some notable differences.

And while you've got your pen and paper handy, make a list of the things you do not like and do not wish to do under any circumstances. If you love to write, but absolutely hate time constraints and working to meet deadlines, a career in journalism is not for you. Fiction or poetry writing on your own time would be a better use of your gifts.

Another thing to look at is the kind of lifestyle you want to lead. Several factors come into play at this stage in the game:

- How important are money, status, and upward mobility to you?
- Is it important to you to have a flexible job, giving you freedom to pursue volunteer activities, hobbies, or to concentrate on family responsibilities?
- Do you view work as the primary fulfilling task in your life, or should it simply pay the bills and leave you some spare time to pursue more rewarding activities?
- Do you want to settle down in one community indefinitely, or would you relocate if your work required it?

These are all important factors to consider, as the degree to which they are met will significantly affect your level of satisfaction in the career you pursue.

Finally, list any goals or aspirations you may already have. Perhaps you've always wanted to coach basketball. Or maybe your family owns a business that you've been waiting to join. Be sure, however, to recognize the difference between dreams and aspirations. Most of us have probably at least occasionally dreamed of becoming famous professional musicians, actors, or athletes, but few of us have ever aspired to such things. Are your vocational goals and aspirations things you could realistically attain or just fun things to think about when you can't fall asleep at night?

Once you've made all your lists, take a break and let your subconscious do some synthesizing work. Come back to your lists a few days later and read them over. Are there some general directions beginning to emerge? If you've always excelled in sciences, you enjoy working with people, and you don't mind a fairly all-consuming work life, a career in the health sciences may be something to examine more thoroughly. If, however, science is a strength of yours but you prefer to work alone and have a fairly regular schedule, a research vocation may be more up your alley. Discuss your lists and analysis with close friends, your parents, or your pastor, and jot down any insights that emerge.

The services of a career counselor, whose job is essentially to walk you through the processes outlined in this chapter, could also be enlisted at this stage. If you are a student, contact your student services department for more information about career counseling. Many educational institutions offer services of this nature at minimal or no charge for their students. Your local or regional government employment agency should also be able to refer you to public or private programs where career counseling is available. Most career counselors are also able to offer advice on resume preparation, interview skills, and other job-hunting essentials. You may find the knowledge and objectivity of such a professional to be a real asset in your quest for meaningful work.

The business section of your local public or university library can also be of great assistance. Many career-planning manuals have been published in recent years. Two that I would highly recommend are *What Color Is Your Parachute?* by Richard Nelson Bolles (Ten Speed Press, updated annually) and *Jobsmarts for Twentysomethings* by Bradley G. Richardson (Vintage Books, 1995). These books provide more detailed reading and suggestions for the steps I have outlined in this chapter. *What Color Is Your Parachute?* has an entire section with a host of charts and worksheets to help you zero in on your most marketable gifts and skills.

Take stock of the job market

Now that you have a sense of your own gifts and interests, it's time to take a look at what kind of work is out there for you. The two books I just mentioned both contain lists of existing occupations, the skills or interests you should possess if you're interested in pursuing them, and the kind of training required to get these jobs. Another helpful book is *Careering and Re-Careering for the 90s* by Ronald L. Krannich (Impact Publications, 1993), which includes chapters on taking advantage of emerging trends in the job market and the economy. (All of these books are geared specifically for the United States public. Canadians wanting job-prospect information more specific to the Canadian scene can obtain this information through Statistics Canada at your local public library or Employment & Immigration office.)

The information these resources contain about the present state of the job market for a particular occupation as well as the future outlook can be very helpful in making a realistic career decision. These books can also be sources of information about new occupations you may never even have heard of, since our rapidly increasing technology seems to create new occupations at about the same rate as it makes old ones obsolete.

Evaluating the competitiveness of the job market for a particular occupation is becoming more of a concern. The state of the economy in both Canada and the United States currently means that there are lots of applicants for few job openings. Therefore, employers can afford to be selective in their hiring. Although the competition factor shouldn't make you avoid an occupation altogether, it is something to keep in mind. How well do you handle pressure, competition, and rejection?

Competition also occurs in training for certain occupations. Many professional colleges and technical schools have quotas for their programs, thus creating competition even to get the training to qualify for a job. As public funding for higher education declines, training programs become more and more inaccessible due to restricted entry and rising tuition costs. Once again, you don't want the current state of the educational system to dictate what you do with the rest of your life, but you do want to be realistic.

If researching prospective occupations does enable you to set your sights on a particular occupation, or at least a general field of study or training, it's a good idea to map out what hoops you will need to jump through to get from your current state to the occupation you have chosen. Once again, refer to the earlier mentioned career-planning guides, which can tell you what training is required.

Talk to people already doing the stuff

People currently employed in the profession in which you are interested are a great source of information. They'll give you the human angle to add to the knowledge you have already gleaned from books. Is the profession really what the books say it's cracked up to be? Does the current situation measure up to what the books predict? For example, your career-planning guide may tell you that you need at least a bachelor's degree in psychology to be a marriage and family therapist, but the marriage and family therapists out there might tell you that you shouldn't hope to find work or clients until you have a doctorate. Information of this sort may affect your decision to pursue a particular profession.

People employed in your profession of interest may be able to tell you some of the "ins" for gaining training or experience in your field. If you are interested in becoming an auto mechanic, a garage owner may be able to hook you up with another garage owner looking for some part-time, unskilled help where you could learn the ropes. A physical therapist may be able to suggest places where you could volunteer to learn more about the kind of work physical therapists actually do.

People in a particular profession can also tell you which schools or training programs are considered most reputable in your field, or what qualities or experiences aside from formal training employers tend to look for in potential employees. This will provide you with information to make a more informed career decision, and give you the tools to prepare yourself in the best way possible for the career you do choose to pursue. Thorough preparation is the best way to beef up your chances of landing that job you really want.

What if you still don't know what to do with your life?

For a variety of reasons, a thorough searching may still leave you without a clear choice of an appropriate occupation. Maybe you have a wide variety of interests. Maybe you are experiencing some other stressors in your life, such as family or other relationship problems, which are making it difficult for you to focus on a career decision right now. Maybe you feel you simply don't have a need right now to choose a particular occupation, and are content to occupy yourself with whatever jobs or other opportunities seem to come up.

There is nothing wrong with deciding not to decide on a particular occupation if you feel that you're just not ready yet to do so. Unfortunately, others may not be so supportive of such seeming indecision.

Parents are notoriously concerned about the future of their children. This parental concern can translate into pressure toward a premature career decision. Assure your parents that it's actually unwise to spend a lot of money (often their money) preparing for a job that you're not sure you really want and may never actually have. Assure them that it is possible to lead a purposeful existence without actually preparing for a particular job.

Of course, your parents will be much more convinced that you are leading a purposeful existence if it actually looks and is purposeful. If you are skipping classes, showing up late for work, or lounging on the family room couch "job-hunting," your parents' concern about your lack of direction may be justified. But if you're upgrading some high school classes to create a few more occupational options, keeping up with a

good core of liberal arts classes that are required for a
variety of professional colleges, or simply working
somewhere to pay your own bills and enjoying a bit of
a relaxed schedule after twelve intense years of school,
it shouldn't be too hard to convince your parents that
your time is being spent in meaningful ways.

Your parents may not be the only ones hounding you
about your occupational future. Instructors or profes-
sors may have a bias toward students who know what
they're going to do with their lives. Employers usually
want to know if you're working for them just for now,
or if you're in for the long haul. Well-meaning adults at
family gatherings, church gatherings, and a host of
other places will often initiate conversations with questions like "So, what are you doing now that you're out
of school?" Again, the thing to remember is that your
life can be purposeful and meaningful without a specific long-range goal in mind. If you're using your time
as an opportunity to explore interests or to sort out significant issues in your life, there's no need to be apolo-
getic.

Occupational paralysis

It's not okay to avoid a decision that definitely does
need to be made. Deference can eventually become
avoidance, and sooner or later you may fall into a sort
of "occupational paralysis." The job you've worked at
for the last three years "just to pay the bills" is little
more than a tedious routine. You've lost all motivation

to do well in your classes because you're not sure why you're taking them. When people ask you what you want to be doing in five years, you have absolutely no idea. Your life feels directionless and meaningless, and the greatest compulsions you experience are to watch TV, avoid "responsible" people, and sleep in.

If your depression stems from your lack of certainty about your occupational future, it's time to make some decisions. There are legitimate reasons to postpone a career decision. Plain old ordinary fear and uncertainty are legitimate reasons for awhile, but if fear and uncertainty are paralyzing you, muster up all your courage and determination, go back to the beginning of this chapter, and start the process.

The good news is that you don't need to arrive with complete certainty at the occupation that's right for you to overcome your depression. Even the process of collecting the information you need to make a decision will help you feel better. Just do something, start somewhere, and let the energy you get from that beginning propel you forward. You are the only person who can initiate the process.

Am I really going to do this for the rest of my life?

It's safe to assume, based on current statistics, that you will change occupations at least three times in your adult life—at least three times. Changing occupations is possible, even common, and probably healthy as well. If your future involves a spouse and children, getting more training or switching jobs will likely require a little more patience, planning, and compromise than it will if you are single, but it's still possible. Few of us will find ourselves at age sixty-five retiring from the same job or even the same kind of job we first landed.

Dealing with the McJob

What if it doesn't work out? In the novel *Generation X*, Douglas Coupland describes a McJob as "a low-pay, low-prestige, low-dignity, low-benefit, no-future job in the service sector. Frequently considered a satisfying career choice by people who have never held one" (Douglas Coupland, *Generation X*, St. Martin's Press, 1991, p. 5). McJobs are the jobs you settle for when you can't get the jobs you want.

Unfortunately, more and more young adults, regardless of their training and aspirations, are finding themselves in McJobs. In some situations this is due to a depressed economy that makes education inaccessible to a greater segment of the population, and that creates a small, highly competitive job market. Only those who are exceptionally talented in a particular area get the training and the subsequent jobs. In other situations it is due to an individual's unrealistic assessment of their own abilities. Convinced they're talented in an area where they really aren't, they get the required training but find themselves unable to land a job.

If you find yourself in a McJob, take a good, hard, and honest look at what put you there. If at all possible, involve a person who knows you and your chosen field of work well and who is willing to be brutally honest with you in this process. Are you genuinely good at and suited for the work you have chosen, but unable to get a job in your field because of few openings and stiff competition?

If this is the case, you have several options:

- Ride out your McJob until the job market changes, doing extra courses or volunteering to remain current in your field of work in the meantime.

- Maybe you have all the necessary skills, but simply aren't able to sell yourself to potential employers. Take a course or get some counseling to beef up your job-hunting skills. Contact your government employment agency for more information about such services. Or visit the library. I discovered the business section in my local library contained dozens of manuals on resume writing, interviewing, and other job-hunting skills, many of which were occupation specific. A good generic one to consult is *The Complete Resume & Job Search Book for College Students* by Bob Adams (Bob Adams Inc., 1992).

- Do a more thorough search of the job market for openings related to your field of expertise for which you might be qualified (e.g., tutoring opportunities for a teacher, private counseling openings for a social worker).

- Consider applying for volunteer work with a development agency such as Mennonite Central Committee. These agencies shouldn't be looked upon as employment services, but if you have a genuine willingness to serve, they usually have openings for people with a variety of particular skills.
- If your training lends itself to such a leap, open your own business! Ever-increasing numbers of people are choosing to make a living through self-employment or contract work. Again, your government employment agency can provide you with counsel on the feasibility of such an enterprise and the necessary procedures for initiating it.

If none of these options yields any more satisfying work, remind yourself that this is more a reflection of the current economic situation than your particular worth or giftedness. And if the prospect of staying in your McJob indefinitely is a little too much for you, consider retraining in another field that interests you and that is currently enjoying a little healthier job market.

But what if you discover that you aren't as well suited to your chosen area of work as you had first thought? Again, remind yourself that this is not a reflection of your particular worth or giftedness. Just because you aren't gifted in a particular area doesn't mean you aren't gifted in another area.

Admitting that an occupation you were genuinely interested in and for which you thought you possessed the necessary gifts really isn't for you is painful. There's no getting around that. Recovering from this will involve efforts on your part both to regain your self-esteem and to re-evaluate your gifts and interests. The prospect of beginning another course of training can be discouraging. Again, consider enlisting the services of a career counselor to provide you with support and objectivity in this process. If your hard work and heartache eventually lands you in a job in which you will excel and feel satisfied, the journey will be worth it.

Your job is not your life

As mentioned earlier, in our society we tend to equate people's identities with their jobs. Many individuals in our society will determine the amount of respect and worth they should grant you by the occupation you hold. This creates additional pressure to make the "right" career decision.

Your life is ultimately about finding personal satisfaction by living faithfully as a Christian. That means choosing a lifestyle that is consistent with Christian ideals like justice, equality, peace, and love. It is more important for your occupation to remain consistent with these ideals than for it to provide you with a measure of success and status in the eyes of society. You don't have to be wealthy or successful to live a faithful life as a Christian. In fact, it might be easier if you aren't. You also don't have to be a pastor or a relief worker or a social activist to genuinely express your faith in every aspect of your life.

What you do need to do is to take advantage of everyday opportunities to do the work of God's kingdom, between nine and five or afterwards. That can be as simple as smiling at the person you're serving at McDonald's, and as life-changing as being willing to put your job on the line rather than compromise your faith. How much money you make or how much status society grants you for doing these things is immaterial. Personal satisfaction and integrity are far more important than that. Don't let your life become a slave to your job.

 QUESTIONS FOR DISCUSSION

1. How strongly do you feel your current or future occupation is equated with your identity? Is this frustrating or satisfying for you?

2. Contrast the stories of Joseph (Genesis 39:1-6) and John the Baptist (Matthew 3:1-6; 14:1-12). Both strove to be faithful to God in their occupations. For one it brought prosperity and a long life. The other lived as a peasant and nomad and eventually lost his head.

- **Can you think of modern counterparts to these biblical characters?**
- **How do you reconcile these very different stories with the leading of the same God?**

- What challenges or lessons do these biblical stories hold for you?

3. If you worked for a financial institution that you discovered made its primary investments in a corporation you believed had very unethical or oppressive practices, what would you do? Invite any group members who have faced faith challenges at work to share them.

4. Are there specific things the church can do to encourage and support its young adults in an age where the job market often devalues and depersonalizes them?

5. Life on a Shoestring: How to Live for Today and Still Save for Tomorrow

If people who know me find it amusing that I've written about time management, they may find it even more amusing that I've also written a chapter on financial management. Those sayings about money burning a hole in your pocket or slipping through your fingers could have been invented to describe me. Financial management has often meant surviving to the next paycheque when my bank balance had dropped pretty close to zero within a few days of the previous deposit. Nevertheless, I have compiled some financial-management advice that I hope you will find worthwhile—some based on my own hard-learned lessons and some gleaned from people who know more about financial management and do it better than I do.

Why bother?

There are at least two reasons for attempting to manage finances. First of all, for a lot of us it takes some effort to make finances stretch to cover all the things we want them to cover. Taking the time to do some thinking and planning ahead of time increases the chance of having the necessary funds available when and for what we need them.

But this chapter isn't just about planning to get the most for the dollar. Financial management is a justice issue. And justice issues should be of concern to those who claim to follow Christ.

Contrary to what our capitalist North American society would have us believe, the world has a limited amount of resources, financial or otherwise. These resources are easily sufficient to sustain the current global population, but are distributed very unequally. To dramatically simplify a very complex situation—though there is enough to go around, some people have too much, leaving too little for others. Therefore, the high standard of living typical in North America can be maintained only if people in numerous other countries continue to live in poverty. And the choice to maintain or change this unjust system rests with us because we hold a vast amount of the world's economic resources and control where they go.

Financial management is as much about attitudes as it is about finances. As long as we continue to view our money as our own, we will perpetuate the injustices of economic distribution. If we begin to view our money as one of the many gifts we receive from God—to be used, like other gifts, to bring about God's reign—we will begin to make choices that will encourage a more just distribution of economic resources. Trying to live more simply is one of the first choices you can make toward this end.

This is the essence of Christian stewardship—a concept that is much larger than simple financial management, one that will take a lifetime of commitment and practice to learn. So there's no time like the present to start. And I hope you will embrace a simple lifestyle, not just for now as a way to stretch summer earnings over two semesters of study or an entry-level salary over all the expenses of independent living. I hope you will embrace it for life, as an essential expression of your commitment to Christ and the well-being of all people.

Where do I start?

Make a budget. Making and sticking to a budget are essential to good financial management.

You may feel that a budget is unnecessary, since you only have enough money to pay the necessary bills anyway. Let me persuade you, using a few examples, that making a budget is still useful. Perhaps you own a vehicle that you use to drive to school or work. By sitting down and calculating what it costs you to drive your car to work or school, park it, and drive it home again, you may discover that it would be more economical for you to take a bus—something you never would have discovered had you continued to drive your car, chalking it up as a "necessary" expense. Or maybe you spend a dollar per page to have your essays typed by someone else because you don't own a computer. Figure out all the costs, and you may discover that over the course of your schooling, you will shell out enough money to your typist to have bought a reasonable secondhand computer for yourself.

Of course, the convenience of having your own car may be worth the extra money it costs you. Or maybe you are techno-phobic, and spending money on a typist is more attractive than spending money on a computer. These are valid reasons to spend your money the way you do and point to one of the fundamental reasons for making a budget. We all make choices about spending our money—even when we feel we are only paying the bills—based on our personal preferences and assumptions. Making a budget forces us to sit down and look at the big picture, seeing what options our preferences and assumptions may cause us to overlook.

So how do I do it?

Much of the information in this section is based on a book that I have found to be very helpful: *How to Survive Without a Salary* by Charles Long (Summerhill Press, 1988). Long advocates making an annual budget, since it allows you to do long-range planning and account for expenses that only come up occasionally. Here's how to do it.

1. *Look at what you earned and spent last year.* Take a piece of paper. Divide it into six columns, using the headings below. List all the things you spend your money on in the left-hand column, grouping them into appropriate categories, like groceries, textbooks, or donations. Remember, we're looking for the big picture, so be exhaustive. This means including saving plans as a category, since we're trying to account for every penny that passed through your fingers last year.

Category	Weekly (x 52)	Monthly (x 12)	Annual	Special	Annual Total for Each Category

Now start filling in numbers in the appropriate columns. Groceries would probably be a weekly expense; bus pass, a monthly one; and car insurance, an annual one. Things like buying a new bike are Special expenses, since you don't expect to incur them every year. Use receipts, canceled cheques, credit-card statements, or anything else you have on hand to make these numbers as accurate as possible. When you have a number for every category, multiply each figure by the appropriate amount (e.g., multiply weekly expenses times 52) to get an annual figure for the Total column. Add up all the numbers in your Total column, and that total should more or less equal last year's annual income, unless you've forgotten an expense category.

2. *Project next year's expenses and income.* Now that you have an idea of where your money has gone in the past, it's time to look ahead. Take two more sheets of paper. Divide one into the same six columns as above, and draw up a second with headings similar to these:

Anticipated change in budget from last year (+ or -)

Expense categories I can drop this year

Expense categories I will need to add this year

Special expenses/projects I anticipate or would like to undertake

Items/projects I would be willing to pass up

Again, note the frequency—weekly, monthly, annual, or special—after each category.

Tackle the "anticipated changes" worksheet first. Employ some common sense and fill in the first two categories. Think ahead carefully, creating as complete a picture of the next year as you can. Account for any changes taking place. If you're moving out of your parental home, add categories for rent, groceries, and utilities. If you've just finished a training program and don't plan on starting another, drop the tuition category. Anticipate any special expenses. Have your Birkenstocks finally fallen apart, necessitating their replacement? Will you be moving from Los Angeles to Winnipeg, requiring you to purchase winter boots and a block heater for your car?

After finishing this step, do a draft run on your budget and compare your expenses to your projected income, just to have a clearer sense of the options available to you in the next step.

Now is the time to take a look at the choices available to you. Is there something you would really like to do, like sign up for that study tour to Colombia or buy a new computer, that would be possible if you reallocated some of your spending? Are there places where you could cut back on your consumption? Do you really need football season tickets, or could you live with just going occasionally? Note these possible changes in the final two categories on your worksheet together with a realistic dollar amount.

With a realistic list before you of the things you need to spend money on and places you could make some changes, think hard about the choices you're making and fill in your budget sheet. This is where the rubber of Christian stewardship hits the road of choice and action. Where can you begin to live more simply? Remember, most things aren't as necessary as we think they are, most things don't need to cost as much as we think they do, and most of the people in the world will benefit from even our small efforts to live more simply. So be creative, be determined, and make a choice to start somewhere. The rewards will show up in your budget and your world.

Don't, however, assume you can change your lifestyle overnight. If new clothes are a weakness of yours, don't assume you can go all of next year without buying any, donating all the money to church instead. Simple living is a noble goal, but striving for it needs to take our humanity into account. Smaller changes over a longer period of time tend to be more successful, just like losing weight slowly is more effective than crash dieting.

3. *Compare and adjust.* Once you've filled in your budget worksheet, add up your Totals column and compare it to your projected income. If the former is less than the latter, you have the freedom to make some more decisions about your surplus. Save it? Blow it? Donate it? Just don't forget that the same principles of Christian stewardship apply to surplus income as to budgeted income.

If your projected income is lower than your projected expenses, you also have choices to make. Take another hard look at your budget. Are there some options for cutting back that you still aren't seeing? Consider nothing sacred. Rent isn't a given—you can move. Utilities aren't a given—you can use less water and electricity. Making these decisions probably won't be all that pleasant, but it's probably more unpleasant to live all year wondering when the cash will run out.

4. *Make it stick.* More young adults find themselves looking for ways to pare expenses than to deal with surpluses. Simple living is sometimes more of a necessity than a choice, which can make it feel a little oppressive. Here are a few suggestions to improve your attitude and your chances of survival on a modest income.

Living More with Less by Doris Janzen Longacre (Herald Press, 1980) and *How to Survive Without a*

Salary are two books with practical suggestions for creative and just ways to spend and save money. Get your hands on one or both of these books (libraries, pastors, and Mennonite Central Committee offices are good places to try) and check them out.

An important underlying principle to keep in mind: Be creative. The most readily apparent solution to any situation is almost always the most expensive one, which often means it's also the most oppressive to others and the environment. Creativity means questioning your assumptions (does name-brand spaghetti really taste better?), learning from other people (how did my grandparents or my friend from El Salvador puree their soups without a Braun hand mixer?), recognizing your own skills can be a substitute for money (maybe I could learn how to change the oil in my car), and never considering any option out-of-the-question (who says I can't make a bike from reclaimed pop cans?!). Cultivating creativity opens up a whole new world of options and is a lot more fun than just plain old saving money.

Take advantage of the support and resources of your church and social communities. Talk to people whose lifestyles and financial decisions you respect and ask them how they do it. Use a "buddy system." Invite a few friends to make a tough financial decision together with you and help each other stick to it. For example, if the gang regularly goes out for supper, consider taking turns hosting potlucks as an entertainment alternative. Keep your ear to the ground for opportunities to get involved in shared housing or other cooperative arrangements like car-pooling. Involving your community in your financial decision making in this way will not only encourage you in your efforts to live more simply; it will also enrich your life by fostering new relationships and deepening old ones—a cheap and healthy alternative to many of the ways society encourages us to make our lives complete.

Other things to think about

If this whole financial management thing doesn't look overwhelming enough already, there's more.

1. *Charitable giving.* Many young adults feel they don't have a lot of cash to spare for charitable causes. Isn't your contribution to church and other charities through time and commitment enough? Well, yes and no. It certainly is a valuable contribution, and no one would ask you to give money instead. But maybe you can do both. If we decided it was important enough, a lot of us could make some different choices about spending our money that would free some up to share with people and organizations who need it. You know the reasons for using our money to bring about justice and the excuses for not doing it. This is an invitation to trade excuses for reasons.

This doesn't mean you should give your money to anyone and everyone who asks for it. Charitable organizations differ in the ways they run their programs and allocate the funds they receive. Find out as much as you can about an organization before you donate. Does your money go where they say it's going? Do they carry out their service in a spirit with which you feel comfortable? Do they do work you deem to be of importance? Ask questions. Generosity is admirable. Gullibility is not.

2. *Loans and credit cards.* I used to think that loans and credit cards were hard to get. A few loans and credit cards later, I realize I was wrong. The truth is that if a financial institution can be even reasonably assured that you will pay the money back, they are more than happy to lend it to you. Their motivation can be summed up by one small word—interest—not the interest they show in you, but the interest they will make from you.

Financial institutions make a very comfortable living by lending money and having it paid back with interest. So be wary of loans. At the time they are granted, they often seem like "free" money, generously lent to someone in need.

Banks, of course, are eager to enhance this selfless image. Thus, they even have a way of making that interest fee itself seem insidiously harmless, by figuring it in with your regular payments. But ask your loan officer to give you the total interest you will pay on your loan over the repayment period, or to tell you what portion of each payment actually goes toward the principal of the loan and how much of it covers your interest. You will quickly see how much that "free" money is costing you.

Credit cards function in a similar fashion. At first glance, they seem to be nothing more than a convenience—right up there with instant teller machines and fast food. Common credit card wisdom is not to rack up any more charges on your card than you know you will be able to pay off at the end of the month. By paying the total balance monthly, you avoid paying interest, and your credit card purchases effectively cost you no more than using cash (not including the stamp and bank service charge for sending your cheque to the creditor and the annual membership fee for your card—which varies greatly).

Keep in mind, however, that it's much easier and more painless to pay with plastic than it is to pay with cash, because the cost of your purchase isn't so acutely impressed upon you. As a friend of mine once said, "When you use a credit card, you can spend your money twice." Or so it seems. You can put that new shirt on Visa, and still have that $20 bill untouched in your wallet—ready to spend (again) on dinner and a movie after your shopping trip. How convenient—until it comes to the monthly bill.

My advice to you credit-card holders out there is this: If you are going to use your credit card like cash, be aware of your monthly budget for the items you use it for, and keep careful track of your purchases to make sure you are not overspending. Treat your credit

card like you would your chequebook. Enter your budgeted amount for charge transactions at the beginning
of each billing period, and enter each charge at the
time it's made. Stop charging when your balance is
zero. Then, pay the complete bill every month and
avoid those nasty interest fees, which can be in the
neighbourhood of 20 percent! Don't even think about
being tempted by that minimum monthly payment.

If this discipline proves to be too much for you, start
using cash. The effects of spending it are a little more
tangible. Hang on to your credit card for situations and
emergencies when cash just won't do—like when you
need a credit-card number to get a membership at your
local video rental place. Or for that late Saturday night
road trip when the car breaks down and you're in some
town with a motel and a mechanic but no instant teller.
Even emergencies, however, still show up on your
monthly bill. Be ready for them.

3. *Savings.* It never hurts to put a little money aside,
even if it's just a little. Whether you're dreaming of a
trip to Egypt or just protecting yourself against the day
your muffler finally falls off or your bike gets stolen,
putting money away in a savings account on a regular
basis is your best plan.

Many sources encourage a regular contribution of a
portion of your earnings (10 percent is a good guide-
line) to a savings account. If you're getting a regular
paycheque, you can have your bank automatically
transfer this amount from the account into which your

LIVING UNPLUGGED

cheque gets deposited to a savings account. That way
it feels like you never had the money at your disposal
in the first place, and it's not so hard to save it. If
you're a student or a seasonal worker earning most of
your money during one season and spending most of it
during another, budget your money to avoid a zero balance in your account at the beginning of the next earning period. That cushion will come in handy if some
unexpected expenses come up in the meantime—and
they so often do.

If your goal is to save not just for a rainy day but to
fulfill some dream, like buying a car or going on a trip
overseas, try the "material fast" approach (Long, p. 85).
For a predetermined amount of time, budget for essentials only—rent, basic food, and essential bills (like
heat and water)—and pocket the rest—and I mean the
rest. The secret to this approach is the same as crash
dieting—you can give up just about anything—new
clothes, eating out, that great CD—if you know it's
only for a short period of time. In return, you'll be
rewarded with a savings account that grows a lot more
quickly than it would with the standard piecemeal
approach. Just remember to spend the wad on the
dream for which you saved it.

4. *Retirement.* "Retirement?" you ask. And you
thought this book was for young adults! Your sixty-
fifth birthday isn't the time to start planning for your
retirement. Most sources indicate that the social security nets our countries currently provide for those over

75

age sixty-five will be completely bankrupt by the time you reach that age, leaving you to fend for yourself. That's a reason to start thinking about retirement now.

This dire prediction for your life forty years from now may add to the list of worries you feel you must address this minute. That's a reason not to think too much about retirement right now. If you spend your entire working life wondering how you will support yourself the day you are no longer working, stress-induced illness will prevent you from living to see that day.

The number and variety of retirement savings opportunities can be mind-boggling. Currently, government regulations in both Canada and the United States require a portion of any income you receive from an employer to be deducted and deposited with government-administered retirement income security programs. In Canada, this is called the Canada Pension Plan (CPP); in the United States, it's called Social Security. In addition, many employers offer a pension plan as an employee benefit. Most of these require you to contribute a portion of your income, which your employer will match over and above your wage or salary with a certain percentage. Financial institutions offer a wide variety of investment or savings opportunities geared for retirement, such as Registered Retirement Savings Plans (RRSPs) in Canada, or Individual Retirement Accounts (IRAs) in the United States. Most retirement savings options, whether publicly or privately administered, also provide you with income tax breaks.

If you are at a point where you are earning some money on a regular basis, it pays for you to begin checking out your retirement options. This is again because of that little word—interest. The longer you invest your money somewhere, the more interest it will earn. A thousand dollars stashed away when you're twenty will be worth a whole lot more when you're sixty-five than even a couple of thousand stashed when you're fifty.

So talk to a financial advisor whom you trust, explore your options as thoroughly as possible, and go with what you deem the most reasonable. And remember—your purpose here isn't necessarily to retire a millionaire. The simple lifestyle you aspire to during your working years will be much simpler to sustain in retirement than a lavish one.

Is this going to kill me?

In the final analysis, financial management is little more than common sense coupled with a little restraint and some principled and creative thinking. It shouldn't be stressful, depressing, or oppressive. Almost all of us have the financial resources we need, if we just do a little planning and make a few wise choices. And even if you seem to be making more choices not to do things than to do them, life can still be fun. Developing your creativity and resourcefulness can provide you with longer-term satisfaction than the more immediate gratification of material gain. So take heart. This won't kill you. If anything, creatively stretching the financial resources you have available to you will make your life a little richer.

QUESTIONS FOR DISCUSSION

1. Is the way you spend your money really a justice issue? If you spend your time and energy working for social justice, isn't that enough?

2. Assuming that most of us can do with less money than we are accustomed to spending, do you agree that donating money to charitable causes is a requirement for all Christians? Are there alternatives that are justifiable in particular situations?

3. What are some concrete changes you can make in your lifestyle or approach to financial management that would make your resources in this area go a little further? Share your budget worksheets with the group to tap their communal accountability and resourcefulness.

- Have everyone share one or two of their favourite money-saving tips.
- Have each person share the area of financial management or simple living they struggle with the most. Brainstorm together for solutions or ways the group can be supportive.
- Commit to a discipline (e.g., reducing entertainment spending by 25 percent) or a project (e.g., supporting a refugee family) as a group. Make sure you agree on mechanisms for monitoring your progress toward your goal.

6. "To Do It or Not To Do It" and Other Questions

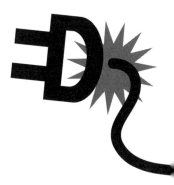

"**D**ating and relationships" used to be the code words for Sunday school or Bible study discussions that just might be about sex. Nowadays, the code word for such discussions is "sexuality," that all-encompassing term that could mean you are in for a session on anything from gender stereotypes to basic reproductive education.

Sexuality is the sum total of our identity or self-understanding, and thoughts or actions that are affected by the fact that we are sexual beings. This includes a whole realm of stuff from gender differences in socialization to actual sexual desires. Thus, sexuality affects how we perceive our abilities and our self-worth. It affects the way we relate to other people of the same or opposite sex, whether it's in romantic or platonic encounters. And our sexuality also embraces those thoughts and feelings we have that are specifically considered "sexual."

Contrary to popular rhetoric, the fact that our sexuality affects us in a lot of ways doesn't mean that we are first and foremost beings whose primary need is sex. Sexuality is one part of our identity, along with other factors like race, faith, family history, and level of self-esteem. Because of the way all these different identity factors interact, sexuality will affect us in some way all the time, but will never be the only part of our identity that will affect us at particular times. Our major task as human beings is to understand and integrate all these different parts of our identity so that we can function as whole and coherent persons.

A litany of the non-helpful

Obviously, this identity integration task is no small undertaking. When it comes to dealing with sexual identity, and the way your sexual desires fit into the big picture, you are going to have to be discerning about where you turn for guidance. Since most people are very interested in and like to talk about sexuality or experiment with sexual activity, there's a lot of information out there. Not all of it is helpful.

Sexual desires often get blown out of proportion. Judging from media portrayals, most of us are either thinking about or engaging in some sort of sexual encounter most of the time. Our society creates the message that sexual desires are the most pervasive and most demanding part of our identity. Satisfying your sexual urges is the chief good that you should pursue in life.

Sexual desires or needs are indeed a powerful force in our lives—but so are our needs for food, shelter, emotional intimacy, and finding some purpose for our lives. There's nothing wrong with seeking appropriate ways to satisfy each of these needs. Problems arise when a particular need is isolated from the rest. Then you start to make decisions based on one particular need without taking the rest of your identity into consideration. You forget who you are as a whole person and function as a being driven by one particular desire.

Our society encourages this kind of isolation of our sexual needs from the rest of our identity by elevating and exaggerating them. This encourages the setting of some rather skewed priorities. Making the fulfillment of your sexual desires the driving force in your life sets you up to make some unhealthy decisions in this area and to miss out on some other important things.

Unfortunately, the church isn't always all that helpful either. If society has isolated our sexual needs from the rest of our selves by exaggerating them, the church has been guilty of the same by degrading sexuality, by equating sexual desires or activities with guilt. If you have the urge to do anything more than give someone a peck on the cheek, you'd best go take a cold shower and reflect on the purity of your thoughts and action. Take this approach a little too far, and you end up as people who can't view any kind of sexual encounter positively, even in settings the church does deem appropriate, like marriage.

So what's a person to do?

Where's the healthy middle ground here? Start by reminding yourself again that sexual intimacy is just one of your needs. Your personhood won't evaporate if you don't get any, nor will you magically become a whole and satisfied person if you do. If you can keep in mind that sexual intimacy is neither bad nor the ultimate good, you are in a better position to be able to make some healthy decisions about your own sexual desires.

Decisions about sexual activity should always be made with your whole person in mind. Do you genuinely care for the other person? How committed are you to your relationship? What are the small voices in the back of your head saying? Are you considering something that might compromise your self-respect or integrity, or that of the other person? How does your faith speak to your decision? Although it's often tempting to leave the constraints of faith or other personal values behind in the heat of the moment, you can never run away from these things forever. Isolating decisions about sexual activity from decisions you have already made about your relationship with the other person, your own personal standards, and your faith is the point at which sexual intimacy becomes both painful and sinful.

Sex is something good that God created. Like all the other things God created, it has a place and a purpose. The Bible makes some pretty unequivocal statements about the act of sex itself being reserved for one man and one woman in a marriage relationship (e.g., Genesis 2:23-24, Deuteronomy 22:22-29, Proverbs 5:15-20). Consequently, biblical teachings regarding sex are often interpreted to us by others as a joyless list of do's and don'ts.

The reality is much broader than this. God's Word is given to us for the purpose of helping us become the people God created us to be—whole people in right relationship with ourselves, each other, and God. Biblical teachings about sexual activity need to be interpreted within the context of biblical teachings regarding love, intimacy, and how we are to treat others. In his letters, Paul refers many times to the nature of true Christian love and admonishes his readers to live by these standards. Our relationships are to be characterized by respect, kindness, compassion, righteousness, and peace (Romans 12:9-21; 1 Corinthians 13:4-7; Colossians 3:12-17).

Put into this broad context, what the Bible teaches about sex is what a lot of psychologists would agree makes for the healthiest decisions about it. Sex should never abuse power. Sex should never be used to manipulate or hurt another person. Sex is not a measure of self-worth. Sexual activity should never go beyond the level of love and commitment in a relationship, nor should it be taken as a substitute for genuine caring and emotional intimacy. Behind and beyond these negative admonitions is a whole realm of positive ways of expressing intimacy that are healthy and gratifying—and that are even our responsibility as Christians!

Keeping these things in mind, we can make decisions about sexual activity that allow us the freedom to enjoy this beautiful means of expressing intimacy without guilt. We can be assured that whether or not we are involved in any sexual relationship, we are still valuable and lovable people capable of enjoying a whole range of intimate and satisfying relationships. Most importantly, we can be free from the confusion, exaggeration, and pain regarding sexual activity that so often plagues us and pursue satisfaction in the entire scope of our lives.

What if it's too late?

It would be naive to assume that no one reading this chapter has ever made a decision about sexual activity that they have regretted. Lots of us carry around confusion and guilt about our sexual decisions and actions.

As noted earlier, the Bible is pretty clear about God's intended purpose for the act of sex itself. Therefore, we know what is definitely okay (complete abstinence from all forms of physical intimacy) and what is definitely not okay (premarital or extramarital sex). But all the area in between, where the Bible makes no direct admonitions and where a lot of things can happen, is open to interpretation. Not being sure how we should feel about activity in this in-between area, many of us end up feeling guilty.

If you have made a decision about sexual activity that you regret, for whatever reason, you don't have to repeat it. People have a tremendous tendency to view themselves as incapable of making better choices after making even one regrettable one, which tends to cause them to continually make the same regrettable one. Everyone is capable of making good decisions. It may require more knowledge and effort, and you need to believe it is possible, but it is possible.

More importantly, forgiveness is always possible. A lot of people tend to view what they feel are their sexual sins as somehow worse than their other sins and therefore beyond forgiveness. Many people have also been sexually abused, causing them to feel guilt and responsibility for actions that were beyond their control. But the truth is that God forgives everything and heals all wounds. It's more difficult to feel this on a personal level than it is to know it on an intellectual level. Guilt is a tremendously deep-seated and pervasive emotion. But God's love and forgiveness are powerful. God can heal wounds, and God can give you the strength and self-respect to make better choices or to believe in your worth as a person. If you need the help of a pastor or counselor to regain your belief and trust this promise, seek that help. No one deserves to feel guilt or shame for their entire lives.

What if I'm gay?

If you are or suspect you are homosexual, your struggle with sexuality will be more difficult than that of your heterosexual peers. Much of society has proclaimed your sexual orientation as unnatural, and much of the church has proclaimed it sinful. Fine for me to say that you should make choices that allow you to integrate your identity—but where does that leave you when society tells you that you must choose between your "normal" self and your "deviant" self, or when the church tells you to choose between your "religious" self and your "sexual" self?

Many Christian denominations have officially declared homosexual activity as a violation of biblical teaching. Many denominations have also committed themselves to further dialogue and to openness to the Holy Spirit's guiding toward truth and repentance. God calls us to be whole persons—persons of integrity—and for the church to be a body of integrity. Honest sharing, compassionate listening, and careful reflection are necessary for this.

It is unfair to expect homosexual persons to make their sexuality a public matter, which is what happens when homosexuality remains a topic of churchwide discussion, when that is not the expectation of heterosexual people. However, I hope that you can find creative ways to share your struggle in the church that will invite all of us to a deeper exploration of our own sexuality and our own understanding of truth. And I pray that the church will have ears to hear your story.

What do you really want from the church?

As I write all of this, I struggle with the two conflicting voices of young adulthood I find ringing in my head. In one ear, I hear the voices of many young adults who are calling for clearer teachings from the church regarding sexuality and many other issues. In the other ear, I hear the voices of many young adults calling for the church to be less bound by restrictive, traditional teachings.

The line between issuing clear teachings and loosening restrictions is a tremendously fine one to walk, even for the most perceptive and progressive of church leaders or institutions. Perhaps it's even impossible. Therefore, I invite you to reflect on what you want to hear from the church regarding sexuality and why. Do you want the Christian church to issue an exhaustive list of sexual do's and don'ts? If so, are you prepared to submit yourself to it? Do you want the church to abandon traditional, restrictive teachings because you feel they are unfaithful to biblical teaching? Or are you looking for the church's blessing on decisions you have already made? Your challenges are essential to the ongoing faithfulness of the church, but accountability is also a two-way street. In calling the church to greater faithfulness, you need to be ready to have it call you to greater faithfulness. Open and honest two-way dialogue will draw us all closer to the truth of God.

QUESTIONS FOR DISCUSSION

1. Invite everyone to share their responses to the following questions:
   - Where have you received the most or the most helpful information about sex and sexuality? What did this information consist of?
   - Where have you received the least or the least helpful information about sex and sexuality? What did this information consist of?
   - What questions or concerns do you have about sex and sexuality that have never been adequately addressed anywhere?

Based on your responses, do you agree with the assessment presented here that neither society nor the church have been very helpful in the area of sexuality? What are concrete changes that society or the church could make in the kind of information they present about sexuality or the way they present it that would be more helpful?

2. Here's a group exercise to share opinions about "how far is too far." Designate one end of the room as being "Too far," the other end as "Okay," and the middle as "Depends." Have everyone go to the part of the room that characterizes their response to the items on the following list. Then, have everyone find one other person (from their area of the room or another) and spend one minute discussing together their reasons for their opinion.

   Necking
   Petting above the waist
   Petting below the waist
   Petting with clothes on

Petting with clothes off
Masturbation
Oral sex
Genital sex
3. Revisit the questions raised in the last section of the chapter. What do you want from the church, clearer teaching or fewer restrictions? Is there a way the church could satisfy both concerns?

7. The Church—Love It or Leave It?

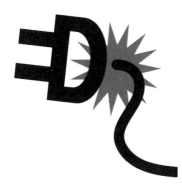

Most Christians will go through at least one period in their life where they feel some ambivalence or confusion regarding their personal faith. This is bound to happen if you spend any amount of time reflecting on your faith. Generations of practical wisdom tell us that more often than not, this faith struggle occurs during young adulthood.

Understanding the generation gap

If every generation of young adults in the church since time immemorial has gone through some sort of faith struggle, it is perplexing that the faith questions and challenges of young adults continue to pose such a difficulty for older adults in the church. You would think this common experience would unite generations rather than divide them.

However, as exhibited in an alarming number of cases, human memory is very short. A certain amount of relief accompanies the completion of any life phase, causing us to forget what it was like to be there or even to disdain those still struggling through that phase (the impatience many young adults have with adolescents is a close-to-home example of this). This phenomenon is commonly referred to as the "generation gap."

Of course, the shortness of human memory isn't the only thing responsible for the generation gap. The time that elapses from when one generation experiences a particular stage of life to when the next does is obviously a huge contributor. The passage of time inevitably brings change. Modern middle-aged adults spent their formative years in a world of different church and societal norms than today's young adults.

The generation that currently holds much of the power in the church grew up in a time when loyalty was a big thing. You picked your name brands, your church, and your spouse, and you stuck with them through thick and thin—or at least the prevailing attitude was that you should. Today's young adults, on the other hand, have grown up in an age that encourages freedom and choice. You choose to eat, wear, or do something because it suits your fancy right now. It if doesn't suit your fancy later today or tomorrow or next week, you can always eat, wear, or do something else.

Obviously, this creates a clash when it comes to church participation. If you grew up in a particular church, older adults may expect you to continue participating in that church simply because it's your church. You, however, may be more interested in attending a church that can relate to your current needs and interests, which may take you beyond the walls of your home congregation or even your own denomination, or maybe even outside the institutional church. Nostalgia and loyalty are nice, but not necessarily sustaining in the face of a major faith upheaval.

The consequences of the generation gap

Of course, the biggest consequence of the generation gap is exactly that—a gap between generations in understanding, in communication, in lifestyle choices, in memory. Somehow, connections just don't get made. Perspectives are just too different, and efforts to find common ground, even as basic as concern for the future of the church, only serve to accentuate these differences.

For example, you may think that all those new ideas you think your church should be discussing and all those suggestions you have for how your church could improve in various areas will be the most welcome thing since padded pews. If there's anything that can bridge the chasm between you and older adults in your church, it's your enthusiastic interest in improving the church you share. You may be surprised.

The older generation may share your concern for the enhancement of church life, but they may not think that discussing new ideas or trying new things is the way to go about it. Church is the place where the "age-old truths of the Bible" are imparted to eager and willing souls. Age-old truths don't usually change too much in one generation. If the quality of faith and life in the church is going to be improved, it will be through improved teaching of these timeless truths.

Remember, generally speaking, human memory is short. Even people who were once young adults urging change and exploration may have settled into some stability they'd like to see preserved. There's a pretty major gap between the need for stability and the need for change.

The purpose of all of this isn't to blame older adults or young adults. I'm simply pointing out that any personal faith struggles you may experience may be compounded by frustration in trying to process these struggles with your church community. And at least some of these difficulties are created by factors beyond your control.

If this is your struggle, you are not alone—it is a common frustration among young adults. It's difficult to feel that you're engaged in an honest, Spirit-led faith struggle only to have others give you the impression that you're anything from just plain annoying to some mild form of the anti-Christ.

Bridging the gap

For several years I have struggled to find ways for young and older adults in the church to recognize the validity of each other's faith experiences and so to strengthen relationships with each other. Along the way, I have been impatient with and misunderstood both groups. However, I have also discovered that there is a good deal more sharing and understanding taking place than I had first thought.

One thing that bridges some of the distance between generations is to share faith through personal story-telling rather than theological discourse. Most people react to a personal statement of opinion by taking sides. You say what you think, and people choose to support or oppose you. The more emotionally charged your statement is, the more emotionally charged people's reactions to it will be. Therefore, eloquent and passionate theological speeches are good breeding grounds for arguments.

But if taking a theological position encourages people to take sides for or against you, sharing a story can do exactly the opposite. People don't have the same tendency to support or oppose a story, because its purpose isn't to initiate debate. A story's purpose is to create common ground, to recall for its listeners a time when they might have experienced similar emotions.

Sharing stories of your faith struggles as a young adult invites people to remember their own young-adult experiences. Even if the specific issues others struggled with as young adults are different from yours, the emotions they experienced are probably very similar to yours. And if you can find and acknowledge that common ground, you've begun to bridge the generation gap.

This doesn't mean that you should never ask questions, make theological statements, or raise issues for discussion. I said earlier that most people's natural response to a statement of opinion is to take a side for or against it. It's also true that people's reactions to a statement tend to be less vehement if they know the person who is making it.

Therefore, the starting point for engaging in constructive, mutual dialogue is building good relationships. And the starting point for building good relationships is finding common ground. So if you want to engage others in your faith struggle, if you want to get into the really good debates, and if you want a time when everybody listens to everyone else and leaves challenged rather than frustrated, do some homework. Start a conversation with someone, not an argument. Tell a story and invite them to do the same. Then, use some common experience as a springboard to discuss an issue. We'd all rather talk with someone who's ready to listen and not just promote their own agenda.

You're an adult too

When you feel strongly about something, it's always tempting to resort to adolescent tactics and go on great tirades. In the past we could do that, but as time marches on, adolescent antics become more inappropriate and intolerable. Learning to communicate as an adult rather than an adolescent is one of the struggles of young adulthood. If you want to be treated like an adult, you've got to act like one. That means taking the initiative to get to know someone, to step outside of your own perspective and see things from another person's point of view. The best way to ensure that other people will do this for you is to make sure you do it for them.

Dealing with "perpetual child" syndrome

What if people simply refuse to see you as an adult? This may be an issue for those of you still involved in the same congregation where you attended as a child or teenager. People still refer to you as "so-and-so's child," seeing you as a dependent being, regardless of your age or experience.

The best tactic here? Prove them wrong. I don't mean maliciously so. Simply make an adult contribution to your church. Volunteer for a committee. Sign up to make coffee. Show up when it's your turn to be a greeter. List your name separately in the church directory. Once again, if you act like an adult, eventually people will treat you like one.

What do you do with people who just won't behave?

Of course, one of the problems with life is that others are self-willed beings just like you. You can't control anyone's behavior but your own. You may be bending over backward to share yourself honestly with other people in your church community and feel that no one is making the same effort in return. You may be acting more mature than most senior citizens and still not feel that you're being recognized as an independent adult. Unfortunately, you can't make other people do or think the things you want them to.

This means that some of you will experience the pain of rejection from your church community, regardless of your best intentions and efforts. Whether it's because your questions are particularly broad or your church's vision is particularly narrow, whether it's because you're too passionate or others are too intolerant, in some cases, acceptance or reconciliation just doesn't take place.

This is a painful, lonely, and disillusioning experience that all too many young adults have. The even darker side of this experience is that those people who give up on church often give up on God as well, since the two are so closely identified in our religious experience. If the church is supposed to embody what God is all about, a church that judges and rejects a young adult pretty much makes God undesirable.

If you are a young adult teetering on the edge of church involvement or faith, I invite you to hang on, or at least to come back and try again later. Unfortunately, due to the human limitations with which we all struggle, the wishes of God and the actions of God's people don't always line up. People will be blinded by tradition. People will be frightened by new ideas or big questions. People will pass judgments on others.

God, fortunately, doesn't fall prey to these human tendencies and limitations. God offers unconditional love, acceptance, comfort, and forgiveness to everyone who seeks it. Many of us hope this outstretched hand will come through a church community. But there are times and places where that just doesn't happen. That doesn't mean that God has pulled out, but it does mean you'll have to look harder or in different places to find the assurance and comfort that God has to offer.

Gordon Aeschliman, a Christian writer and social activist, has written a book entitled *Cages of Pain: Healing for Disillusioned Christians* (Word Publishing, 1991). In it, he describes his own and others' experiences of pain at the hands of institutional religion, and offers healing and hope for those who have experienced the same. Aeschliman has harsh words for the institutional church, but I believe his tough honesty is exactly the voice many disillusioned or frustrated young adults need to hear. I recommend this book to you as a resource to help you in your walk with pain and frustration.

Appreciate the value of wilderness wanderings

Wherever your faith journey seems to be taking you, I encourage you to let it run its course. The future and integrity of the church depends upon your willingness to do so. Our capacity to truly understand the nature and will of God is so limited. We should always welcome new questions and ideas. The only way to come to a greater understanding of God is through greater exploration, and you as young adults have such a contribution to make to the faith community precisely because of your willingness to venture into uncharted territory. If we believe that God really is who God claims to be, we need to trust that God's truth will stand the test of this exploration.

Jesus was a young adult. He shook the religious establishment of his time more than anyone else before or since, and we hold him up as an example because of it. Jesus broke all the rules. He healed on the Sabbath. He fraternized with sinners. He treated women with respect. He questioned religious leaders' blind allegiance to tradition. He challenged the notion that the wealthy and powerful are closer to God. And Jesus wandered in the wilderness for forty days, searching desperately and honestly for God's leading, before he began his public ministry.

Not everyone shares this understanding of Jesus' radical example. But I assure you that breaking with tradition, asking questions, and wandering in the wilderness after the example of Jesus is most certainly a worthwhile exercise. It's the opposite of being lost. It's being on a search. As long as you're searching for a greater understanding of God and God's will for your life, your wilderness wanderings will not be in vain. God is present, even in the wilderness. God will lead you, even in spite of yourself, and you can remind others concerned for the welfare of your soul that this is the case.

 QUESTIONS FOR DISCUSSION

1. Do you believe that the generation gap will recur with each succeeding generation? Or is there hope that some future generations will realize their own part in creating this gap and so be able to eliminate it?

2. How do you feel about the suggestions for communication made in the section on "Bridging the gap"? How much freedom should each of us have to just say what we think, and how much should we constrain ourselves by the possible reactions of others?

3. Consider the following scenario: You have just returned home from four years of studying elsewhere, during which you attended a very dynamic, progressive church. You have chosen to rejoin the congregation in which you grew up and have been asked to lead a young-adult Sunday school class. You want to study a controversial new book by a well-known radical theologian and have approached the Sunday school superintendent about purchasing copies for everyone in the class, using church funds. She does not share your enthusiasm about this book.

In groups of three, role-play this discussion, with one person being the young adult, one being the Sunday school superintendent, and one person observing. After five to seven minutes, ask the observer to indicate what you did well and where the dialogue could have been constructive. This role-play exercise could be repeated using real-life situations the young adults in your group may be facing.

8. Wanting In, Wanting Out—Navigating a Love-Hate Relationship with Your Parents

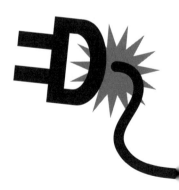

If the generation gap is responsible for creating strain in your relationships with older adults in your church, it's more than likely responsible for strain in your relationship with your parents. Your parents may have forgotten what it was like to be a young adult relating to parents. They may also have forgotten that being a young adult today is not quite the same as it was to be a young adult twenty or thirty or more years ago.

The family factor

In family situations, the already frustrating aspects of the generation gap tend to get complicated by other factors. First of all, there are few places where our patterns of communicating and relating are as ingrained as in our families. We've had our whole lives to develop these patterns, and they're often set by the time we reach the young-adult years.

This means that some of the pointers in the last chapter for adult-to-adult conversations and relationships may be more difficult to implement in relating to your parents. After all, you've related to your parents as their child for twenty or so years. It's going to take a while to develop new patterns of relating as one adult to another.

Add to this the fact that in our families we often don't even relate as nice children to nice adults, and you have the makings of a communication catastrophe. For many of us, our family is the place where we don't have to put on any good fronts to save face or to look polite. If we're feeling cranky, we can go ahead and act cranky. If we're upset with someone, we can be nasty to them. In our families, we can just plain be our true, untouched selves and call 'em as we see 'em. That's what family is all about.

If this pattern of communication is one that is ingrained in your family, it's going to be a challenge to negotiate a civil, adult-to-adult relationship with your parents. You may be willing to make the first move toward fostering good relationships with other adults by acting like an adult, but with your parents? Wouldn't they wonder what was wrong with you?

A sort of a communication schizophrenia may develop. You want your parents to treat you like an adult because, naturally, you are one. On the other hand, you want a sanctuary where you can still be a child, where you don't have to act mature and civilized if you don't feel mature and civilized—where you can just let it all hang out like you've always been able to before. This will confuse both you and your parents, and will be one of the things you have to work at in this renegotiation phase of your relationship.

If your family interactions fall at the other end of the spectrum, characterized by suppressed feelings and very indirect communication rather than blunt honesty, renegotiating your relationship with your parents will also present some challenges. As an adult, you may be struggling to foster more open and honest relationships with others than you experienced in your family. Your efforts to open the lines of communication at home may be met with surprise, suspicion, and confusion.

The generation gap may be further complicated for reasons such as going away from home to school or doing voluntary service. Initially, being away from home may seem like a good way to ease tension between you and your parents. But when you do eventually return home, even for a short period of time, you may find that tension between you has actually increased.

This is likely because you have changed while you were gone, which is no surprise to you but may come as a bit of a shock to Mom and/or Dad. You see, parents are generally used to having some control over what their kids think and do, which means that parents are generally used to kids that more or less think or act the way they do. Parents and children may disagree on minor points like curfews and spending money, but the basic value system is more or less the same, fostering at least some amount of familial equilibrium.

Problems emerge when you leave home and encounter primary influences other than your parents. Mom and Dad are no longer the final authority on everything. This doesn't necessarily mean that you are going to come home disagreeing with everything your parents hold sacred, but it does mean that you won't believe things any longer just because Mom or Dad said they were true.

For you, this transformation will happen gradually over the time you are away. For your parents, however, who only have the privilege of seeing you a few times a year, this gradual change will catch up to them all at once. Not only will they be surprised or dismayed at some of the new ideas you are espousing, they may also be a little hurt that you no longer agree with them on everything. They wouldn't have taught you the things they did if they didn't think they were important things for you to believe. The fact that you're now identifying more strongly with Karl Marx, whom you never even met, than with your own mother or father can seem like an unforgivable slight.

Why bother?

All of this generation gapping may seem a little too overwhelming to tackle. Why should you bother trying to reinstate a positive relationship with your parents, or try to nurture one if there hasn't been one previously?

You may go through a parental avoidance phase. Given all of the above-mentioned factors, that's under-standable and perhaps even healthy. Long-term parental avoidance, however, is not healthy. Your family of origin is far too important a factor in the rest of your life to be ignored. Your ability to develop positive relationships in all other areas of your life rests directly on your ability to develop positive relationships within your family. Pain or non-resolution that persists in familial relationships prevents us from pursuing other committed relationships. Satisfaction and resolution in familial relationships, on the other hand, free us to pursue healthy relationships elsewhere.

How do I do it?

In attempting to negotiate a healthy relationship with your parents, it's important to remember that they are not just other adults. It's useless to ply their sympathy with phrases like "All the other adults I know treat me like I'm their peer. Why can't you just do that too?" Your parents are not all the other adults you know. Your relationship with them will always retain some aspects of a parent-child relationship.

Remember also that unless your parents insist on always treating you like a child, you appreciate the fact that they're your parents and not your peers. In those moments when you just want to be somewhere, even for a short time, where you can avoid responsibility and maturity, you'll be tremendously thankful for Mom and Dad. If you keep in mind that your relationship with your parents will always combine adult and child elements, the rest of these suggestions should begin to make sense.

1. *Your parents are people too.* In the midst of all the change and upheaval going on in your life, it's easy

to forget that changes are taking place in your parents' lives as well. These changes are consuming—menopause, midlife crisis, an empty nest, aging, ailing, or dying parents, etc. Your folks are dealing with some pretty significant stuff that will affect the time or energy they have to relate with you. This doesn't give them an excuse to ignore you or to perpetuate old habits indefinitely, but it does give you a reason to be sensitive to them and their needs. Your parents are people too.

2. *You are an adult.* Just as parents can be people, so children can be adults. As I've already mentioned, we all occasionally like to be in situations where we can just be kids again. Most of us will reserve this kind of behavior for our parents. Parents are also guilty of occasional immature behaviour. Every now and then, your childish behaviour and that of your parents' will coincide.

In situations like this, you can take the first step and act like an adult, since you are one. It's always tempting to wait for our parents to make the first move in this direction, and to blame them if a conversation persists at an adolescent level for too long. You're just as responsible for it as they are. Making the effort to rise above childish ways of communicating will encourage your parents to do the same, and you'll both be happier for it.

A frequent example of this is disagreements many young adults have with their parents over lifestyle choices. Your parents may think you go out too much, you don't spend your money wisely, or you aren't committed enough to your church. Their concerns may often be expressed in dogmatic or demeaning statements like "Why aren't you more responsible with your money?" Such statements often elicit mature responses like "It's my money. I can do with it what I want."

If you find yourself in a pointless and frustrating dialogue such as this one, take a deep breath and plunge into the world of adult communication. Ask your mom or dad why they're concerned about how you spend your money. Make the first move to get past the petty disagreement to the root of the problem. Invite your parents to share their concern about you in a more constructive fashion, and you increase your chances of them trying to understand you when you explain your reasons for your actions.

3. *It can be done.* You need to believe that the time, energy, and emotion you invest in developing a healthy adult relationship with your parents is worth it. A healthy relationship is possible. If your relationship with your parents has always been pretty good, this won't be hard to believe.

However, if you are facing many unresolved issues, unhealthy and deeply ingrained patterns of relating, or resistance from your parents, this process will require steely determination and persistent hope. Don't give up. Don't be afraid to rely on friends or siblings for

encouragement or to seek the support and advice of a
pastor or counselor. The importance of making your
relationship with your parents work cannot be under-
estimated.

The boomerang kid

Due to a variety of societal factors including poor job
markets, low entry-level salaries, and scarce affordable
housing, more and more families are dealing with
boomerang children—kids who leave home only to
return a few months or years down the road.

If you have boomeranged, I refer you to a helpful
and entertaining book, *Twentysomething, Floundering,
and Off the Yuppie Track* by Steven Gibb (Noble Press,
1992). In his chapter "Moving Back Home," Gibb
gives helpful advice on knowing the difference
between using and abusing the comforts of your
parental home, negotiating the everyday details of living with your parents again, dealing with the negative
stigma of living at home, and facing the "demons" of
old patterns of relating. The boomerang situation creates an urgency to negotiate an adult relationship with
your parents that you may have been able to avoid
while living away from home. Be prepared for this and
do not delay in meeting the need. Your sanity and the
sanity of your parents depends upon it.

The continuing saga

There will never be a stage in your relationship where

you can quit expending time and effort. Change in your life, in your parents' lives, and in the world in general will necessitate reworking your relationship from time to time. That's just the way relationships are. The best way you can prepare yourself for this ongoing work is to develop good communication patterns now. If you can learn to talk through things with them in an adult way, changes that come along will be dealt with more smoothly.

This chapter has only skimmed the surface of family/parental issues. There is a lot of dysfunction in families that this chapter has not dealt with adequately. If you are a victim of abuse by a family member, if a difficult divorce or remarriage has complicated your family, or if your family situation is extremely painful or difficult for other reasons, you may want to consider professional help. The resolution of your family situation will affect your ability to develop healthy relationships for the rest of your life.

The Bible contains many stories of dysfunction in families. The parable of the Prodigal Son is a classic tale of a child falling from grace because of his own greed and being restored as a member of his family through his father's acceptance and forgiveness (Luke 15:11-32). Jacob and Esau struggled for the favour of their parents, resulting in Jacob's deception to steal Esau's blessing from their father (Genesis 25:27-34; Genesis 27). Their story also ended in reconciliation, as Esau forgave Jacob when they were reunited at the

Jabbok River (Genesis 32 and 33). The relationship between Rachel and Leah, sisters and both wives of Jacob, was characterized by jealousy and manipulation (Genesis 29:15—30:24). Rachel died in childbirth before the sisters' relationship was healed (Genesis 35:16-20).

The raw humanity of God's people is evident in each of these stories. But we also see evidence of the inbreaking of grace. God's Spirit can move us to leave behind old grudges, to forgive even serious wrong-doing, and to enjoy restored relationships. The scars of hurt never completely vanish, but new layers of love and understanding can be built over them. You deserve to be a satisfied and fulfilled person. May God give you the strength to begin the journey toward restored relationships.

 QUESTIONS FOR DISCUSSION

1. Identify some of the factors that create a generation gap between you and your parents. What are things you can do to bridge the gap?

2. Do you agree that the state of our family relationships affects other relationships to such a significant degree? Why or why not?

3. How might the presence of older or younger siblings affect the way you would negotiate an adult relationship with your parents?

9. Life in a Pluralistic Society: Agreeing to Disagree?

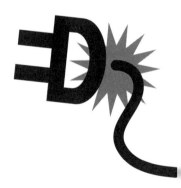

T he world is a complex and diverse place. As our capacity to communicate with and travel to countries around the globe escalates, as the North American population increasingly migrates to large urban centres, and as Canada and the United States become more and more multicultural, things look to be getting even more complex. It's pretty safe to say that your generation will study, work, and live with people of a greater diversity of races, cultures, and mind-sets than any preceding generation.

Living with this kind of diversity is both a privilege and a challenge. Interacting with diverse people provides a tremendous opportunity to participate in the richness and uniqueness of human experience. There is much to learn from the customs, attitudes, and faith systems of those around us. This diversity is also a challenge because of the need to find more positive ways to deal with its struggles than the ones currently being employed. Racial violence and political and religious intolerance are increasing. You have an opportunity, perhaps even a responsibility, to do something about this.

Do your own thing
Young people in North America are already attempting

to remedy this plague of intolerance. A recent Canadian study shows that the majority of Canadian young people believe that "diversity of viewpoint and life-style has become the Canadian way. Ideally it should be appreciated; at minimum, tolerated ... what's right or wrong is a matter of personal opinion" (*Teen Trends*, Reginald Bibby and Donald Posterski, Stoddart Publishing, 1992, p. 98). This finding would likely hold true for the young American public as well.

On the one hand, this trend toward individualism reflects an admirable realism and tolerance on the part of young adults. The world is full of diverse people with diverse opinions. Let's accept and celebrate that rather than trying to deny or change it.

On the other hand, one could ask if this is a truly Christian attitude. As a Christian young adult, should your response to increasing diversity be any different than that of the society in which you live? As a Christian, you have chosen to be part of a group that believes that God—not personal opinion—is the final authority on right and wrong, and everything else, for that matter. Admittedly, however, there is much diversity of opinion even within the Christian church regarding what exactly God deems to be right and wrong.

This is the tightrope many young adults of all faiths are struggling to walk, stretched between accepting and celebrating the diversity of the people around them and holding fast to their own opinions and beliefs.

How will you as a Christian resolve this struggle? You can pull out now and become one of those spineless folk who simply give in to whatever wave of opinion happens to be popular at the moment. Or you can stick with it and struggle a little harder to learn from others and to understand and express your Christian faith with integrity in a world where a lot of people just plain don't agree with you.

The bare facts

We have only one world in which to live. If we're going to live in it at all, we need to learn to live in it together. One way we could get along would be to decide to all be the same. This is highly unlikely.

Another way we could cope with our diversity would be to learn to express our own beliefs and listen to those of others in a way that allows for mutual dialogue and correction. This might be a more realistic possibility than global sameness, but that doesn't mean it would be easy. How can we begin to do this?

Develop a critical worldview

I believe there is some creative and consistent middle ground to be found between "I'm right and everyone else is wrong" and "Everyone can just believe whatever they want to." That ground is found by listening. My friend's mother often says, "God gave you two ears and one mouth for a reason." It's a good idea to listen at least twice as much as you talk.

Listening encourages the development of a critical worldview. A critical worldview is one that recognizes that all of us create our own truth to a greater or lesser extent. None of us—and I mean none of us—receive or possess truth in a pure or unaltered form. All of us interpret particular experiences, dialogues, or teachings through our own particular lens—which is the total of all the other experiences, dialogues, or teachings we have experienced. Listening takes us outside our personal experience and into the experience of another, giving a perspective from which to see how our own worldview is constructed.

Why is this important? If you allow your worldview to remain uncritical, unchallenged, and unaltered, your understanding of God and of truth will be limited to what you experience. You are only one of a vast number of individuals gifted with God's revelation. If you believe that all of creation is good and of God, you need to believe that this is true as well.

This critical worldview is also important because as Christians, our faith journeys are really one long attempt to get beyond ourselves and experience God as God, unaltered by human interpretation or limitations. To not try to do this is to fall prey to the same kind of individualism we talked about earlier, where truth is what each person happens to think it is. You need to develop the ability to hold your beliefs out in front of you, to examine them closely and see if they are as seamless and flawless as you believe them to be.

The paradox of faith is that this quest ultimately has no end. We are human, and, therefore, our attempts to understand God and God's will for our lives will always be colored by our human interpretations and limitations. However, everyone's interpretations and limitations are different. That's why God gave us the gift of community—so that other people's experiences can fill in the holes in our own and expose the fences and defenses we have subconsciously erected that prevent us from being fully human. A diverse world is one of the greatest gifts we have for discovering more about the nature of God, if we are willing to share honestly with others and receive honestly from them.

Of course, in such a diverse world this exchange won't take place only between followers of God. Non-Christians have an important role to play in helping us understand God better. They have a perspective that allows them to point out things like outdated cultural assumptions getting passed off as gospel truth. God is constantly calling us to a greater faith and to new ways of looking at the world. Our interaction with people of other faiths, races, cultures, and mindsets is one of the tools God has provided for us with which to hone our faith.

Keep in mind, however, that a critical worldview is just that— critical. Acknowledging that God is big enough to be revealed to us by all of God's creations doesn't mean that everything everybody says is a revelation of God. Prayer, honest Bible study, and discussion with a discerning faith community are all tools we should use to help us critically evaluate the vast number of new ideas that diverse people will present to us. Being willing to genuinely listen to and attempt to understand the thoughts and ideas of others is not the same as blindly accepting and agreeing with them.

What about evangelism?

Does this mean that you should only listen and never share your Christian faith with anyone? Definitely not. It means you should share your faith at every possible opportunity, inviting others to do the same.

Honest, open dialogue and a genuine attempt to understand another's faith are the healthiest ways to begin any attempt to evangelize. People become interested in Christianity when they encounter Christians whose faith motivates them to take a genuine interest in the lives and beliefs of others. In learning to understand the life and values of another person, you become equipped to share your faith in a way that will meet that person where they are.

Again, there's another side to the story. To truly share the gospel, we need to be confident in our own beliefs. Honest and open dialogue can become pretty scary if we're really not sure about the ideas we're contributing to the dialogue. Do you really know what it means to be a Christian? Do you have a clear sense of why your Christian faith is important to you? If you are wishy-washy about your own faith, conversations with people of other faith persuasions will be just that—conversations. If you are able to share your beliefs with true conviction without disrespecting the other person, you will be engaged in true and faithful evangelism.

Back on the tightrope

If you're spending all your time being so careful to respect other people's beliefs and to see the limitations of yours, aren't you basically just falling back into the individualism we first talked about? No. This is critical dialogue, not individualism, not self-centredness.

Individualism means that everybody can just believe whatever they want to. You have no right to disagree with another person or challenge what they believe because they're just as entitled to their beliefs as you are to yours. Self-centredness means that you believe you have an absolute corner on the truth and everybody else must be lost in the darkness.

Critical dialogue challenges both these worldviews. It's somewhere in the middle. Being willing to engage in critical dialogue means that you feel strongly about your beliefs, strongly enough to share them with others and to disagree with them or challenge them on points where you don't see eye to eye. At the same time, you are willing to be challenged on your beliefs, to have the limitations of your worldview brought to light by the perspective of another. And critical dialogue absolutely requires you to believe in the faithfulness and trustworthiness of God. You must trust that the Spirit of God is at work to bring both parties in the dialogue to greater understanding and faith.

The fact of the matter is that what is right and wrong, how we should live our lives, and how we should view others and the world in general are more than matters of mere personal opinion. We claim to believe in a God who has an ultimate plan for our lives and our world, and who is able to work through all of creation to bring that plan to fruition. By learning from others what they believe to be the truth of God and prayerfully evaluating that, we come closer to both understanding God's plan for creation and bringing it to pass. That's at least part of the reason why God didn't put you on this earth all by yourself. Living together in a world of diversity means stretching yourself to the limit of your abilities to listen and understand and discovering God along the way. It might be frightening, but it's also terribly exciting.

 QUESTIONS FOR DISCUSSION

1. Do you agree with the premise of this chapter? Is there anything wrong with holding to a philosophy of pure individualism?

2. It's sometimes said that Christianity is an exclusive religion because only those who accept Christ as their personal Saviour, regardless of their lifestyle, will be

saved. Do you agree with this statement? How do you feel about sharing this part of your faith with non-Christians?

3. What are ways, other than fostering healthy dialogue between diverse people, that you could work to alleviate intolerance or racism in your community?

10. Ladies and Gentlemen, Boys and Girls: Dealing with the Gender Role Explosion

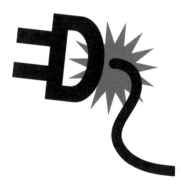

M odern research into human behavior has heralded socialization as a prime mover in our thoughts and activities as human beings. From the time of our birth, society teaches us what is acceptable and what is not, and exerts pressure on us as individuals to conform to these expectations.

Furthermore, many researchers have pointed out that males and females are socialized differently. Societal expectations and pressures are not the same for men and women—something that is impressed upon us at an early age.

More recently, many researchers and writers have claimed that not only are men and women socialized into different roles, they are also socialized into unequal roles. The roles toward which men are steered are accorded more power and worth by society than the roles toward which women are steered. This theory has prompted many individuals to question the fundamental assumptions of our society and the constraints it places on both men and women.

There are many people who seriously question this theory. Many do so on the basis of what could be called "natural" arguments. Men and women tend to take on different roles precisely because there are innate differences between them. Though these natural roles differ by gender, they could not be labeled unequal. Women and men simply fill their rightful place in the natural order.

The great debate

We could probably argue forever about whether gender differences arise because of nature (i.e., innate biological differences) or nurture (i.e., socialization processes) or some combination of the two. We could also argue about whether the value judgments placed on particular roles exist in reality or merely in the perceptions and imaginations of certain men and women. What seems clear is that there are differences, for whatever reason, in the roles that men and women are encouraged or inclined to take on.

More people are expressing dissatisfaction or frustration with these differences. Women have been doing this for awhile. The feminist rhetoric regarding the constraints placed on women because of their gender is likely familiar to you. Many women feel that certain occupations or positions in society are simply not available to them because of their gender. Women who choose professions dominated by men feel they need to be exceptionally talented to prove themselves, while men simply need to be average. And even if a woman lands a job that would "normally" be given to a man, she is paid less for her work. Sexual harassment of women on campus and in the workplace occurs all too frequently. Many women continue to feel that their worth is measured primarily by their physical appearance. Many women continue to fear for their safety in their homes and on the streets.

A newer voice is that of the increasing number of men who are also claiming to be victims of gender-related injustices. In addition to feeling harassed by the critique of feminists, more men are reporting that they are victims of sexual harassment by women. White males feel that they are victims of reverse discrimination when they are unable to get jobs for which they are qualified because of hiring policies that favour women or visible minorities. Men are also expressing frustration with expectations to be strong, rational, or assertive, saying that these societal pressures restrict their freedom to be who they are.

These statements may or may not accurately describe any particular frustrations or limitations you have experienced that could be linked to your gender. But regardless of which side you support in the gender role debate—or if you even take any interest in this debate—the simple fact that it exists and has stirred up such questions and tensions in our society means that it affects your life.

Holding the door open on the issue

The most obvious and pervasive effect of this debate is the simple fact that many of us experience strain in our everyday interactions with the opposite sex. We expe-

rience much confusion and second-guessing in inter-
preting the actions and words of others and wondering
how our actions and words are being interpreted by
them. The simple act of holding a door open for a
friend of the opposite sex can put you through all
kinds of mental calisthenics, wondering and worrying
if your actions will be interpreted the way you intend
them to be. And the action you decide to make has the
potential to generate a heated debate about assumptions of power, position, and worth.

Many of us also face confusion and frustration in
trying to understand ourselves and determine the
course of action for our own lives. How much of the
way we perceive ourselves and our aspirations is influ-
enced by the forces of socialization? And how much of
it is simply who we naturally are?

If nothing else, all this talk about gender roles makes
us aware of our own assumptions about these roles and
how they may or may not match up with other people's
assumptions or our own "pure" nature. Old assumptions just don't seem to cut it anymore, and consensus
on new ones doesn't seem to be readily forthcoming.
That leaves us in limbo. What can we do to ease tension in our interactions with others while this debate
gets sorted out and some new "rules" emerge?

Perception is reality

When it comes to factors, like gender, that affect our
personal sense of the choices and actions that are

available to us and our interpretation of other people's actions in relation to us, it's important to recognize that perception is reality. If we feel that a particular choice does not exist for us, that choice effectively does not exist for us. If we feel that a person's actions toward us were unfairly skewed by gender, a gender-related issue effectively exists.

This is a frustrating phenomenon to deal with, since perception is so subjective and unpredictable. But it's more frustrating to deny that this is so and to try to convince people that they really don't or shouldn't feel a particular way because of what you said or did.

We are all trying to figure out appropriate ways of relating to people of the opposite gender. We're bound to step on toes. This is a reality. Despite our original intentions, the other person's reaction is another reality we have to face.

Listening is understanding

When you find yourself in the middle of a situation like the one just described, you are right smack in the middle of a golden opportunity to shape a new order for gender relations. Listen to what the other person is saying and try to understand what is going on that made them react the way they did. Understanding what creates frustration is an essential part of developing new ways of relating to each other that can avoid these frustrations.

The great underlying issue of the whole gender

debate is the issue of power—who has it and who doesn't. This is precisely the thing that makes the whole process of change in this area so difficult—the people who have power use their power to make sure it stays that way. This is also why so many routine, everyday activities (like holding doors open for people) have become such touchy issues. It's in precisely these everyday situations that much of our worldview and self-perception (i.e., our perceptions about how much power we have in relation to others) is subconsciously, unthinkingly displayed.

If altering the power structure of the entire world is a little much for you to take on all at once, the place to start is in everyday, trivial actions. Pay attention to the assumptions you are making about your status in relation to other people in the way you greet them, address them, look at them, or touch them. Are you assuming that you are more important or less important than the person with whom you are interacting? This exercise will point out assumptions you make about worth on the basis of gender as well as a host of other factors, like race, age, or wealth.

Listening to the feelings of others and examining your own assumptions will enable you to act in ways that empower people—that grant them a sense of autonomy and worth—rather than disempower them. Empowering people effectively eliminates gender biases and limitations, at least in the particular interaction where the empowerment took place.

You are only one person

Never assume that anyone else thinks like you do. Each of us leads a unique life with unique experiences and interactions. Even people experiencing the same event can have wildly different reactions to it.

The moral of the story? Just because you haven't experienced anything that you would call gender discrimination in your life doesn't mean that such a thing doesn't exist. Other people will have experienced the world differently, and their experiences deserve as much a place in the working out of what goes on in our world as yours do. Recognizing the value of each individual's experiences is the first step toward creating a just and equal society. You are only one of many, many individuals. Listen to and respect the voices of others. You'd be surprised at how quickly the debate around gender equality vanishes when that is the case.

 QUESTIONS FOR DISCUSSION

1. Write the following words on a chalkboard or flip chart:

doctor	nurse
aggressive	athletic
musical	emotional
nurturing	teacher
goal-oriented	talkative
pastor	boisterous

Individually, write down whether "male" or "female" comes to mind in response to each of these words. Share your responses with the group. Is there consensus or near consensus on any of the words? As a group, discuss whether our responses to these words arise because there are natural, innate differences between males and females or because society teaches us to expect certain things from males and females.

2. Have two volunteers, one male and one female, role-play each of the following scenarios for the group:

  a. You have been in your current job for almost two years and feel you have really excelled in your work. Therefore, you have decided to approach your supervisor and ask for a raise.

  b. You just had an assignment in one of your classes returned and feel the mark you were given is unfair. You approach your instructor to discuss the issue.

After each role play, have the male and female switch roles and "replay" the scenario. As a group, discuss differences you note, if any, in the way males and females act in positions of more power or less power. Some examples might be differences in use of voice or language, posture, eye contact, or other body language. How would you account for any differences you do notice? Do you agree with those who would argue that men and women are subject to different treatment and expectations in the workplace, classroom, and the church?

11.
Why I Am a Mennonite: What Does Anabaptism Have to Offer Besides This Book?

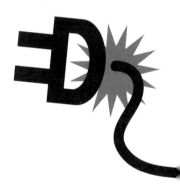

Faith decisions are very personal. They are coloured by our individual experiences of family, church, and the wider world, and the images of hope or struggle each of us see in these places. As mentioned in previous chapters, no two people will experience things in the same way. Consequently, no two people will come to faith or choose to live out their faith in exactly the same way.

Therefore, I can't tell you if you should or why you should be a Christian. I can tell you why I have chosen to be a Mennonite and why the Christian faith continues to support and challenge me in my faith walk. Perhaps there is some common ground between my story and yours that will create some new insights or developments in your own faith journey.

Most of the reasons I have chosen to be a Mennonite reach back to the time before Mennonites were called Mennonites. The Anabaptists, as they were called, were a radical wing of the sixteenth-century religious Reformation initiated by Martin Luther. These Anabaptists were the spiritual ancestors of a number of Christian denominations, including the Brethren in Christ, the Church of the Brethren, and all makes and models of Mennonites.

The early Anabaptists took a number of departures from the religious line taught by Luther, Ulrich Zwingli, and their followers. If you're interested in a complete enumeration of their views, you'll have to take a course in Anabaptist theology. But one of the central theological ideas of Anabaptism is the concept of discipleship. The early Anabaptists taught that becoming a Christian isn't only about saying a little prayer that invites Jesus Christ to become your personal Saviour. Becoming a Christian involves bringing your entire life under the direction of Christ, striving in all ways to model the lifestyle of Jesus.

This concept of discipleship has a number of important consequences, many of which have come to be identified with the Mennonite church. These consequences are what has allowed me to find a spiritual home in the Mennonite church. I firmly believe all of these teachings are at the center of the teachings of Christ, who came to bring not only personal salvation but also social justice.

I am a Mennonite because Mennonites believe in a lifestyle of peacemaking and nonresistance, as exemplified by Christ. By his words and actions, Jesus taught his followers not to take an eye for an eye. Rather, he taught us to turn the other cheek, to love our enemies, and to do good to those who hurt us. These aren't just nice things to do. These are radical concepts that have the potential to transform the world into a place where violence, war, oppression, and hatred are eradicated.

I am a Mennonite who believes in a lifestyle of peacemaking and nonresistance. I believe this not only because I think this is the most faithful interpretation of Jesus' teachings but also because I am concerned for the world in which I live. It is a world that desperately needs people who are willing to work, educate, and live for peace. Being a Mennonite gives me a theology and a community of support from which to do this work.

I am a Mennonite because Mennonites believe in a lifestyle characterized by simplicity. Jesus led a life of material simplicity and spoke unapologetically about the ease with which wealth distances us from God and others. Jesus invited his followers to give up all their possessions and follow him. Jesus spoke of a kingdom where the poor and lowly would be exalted and the wealthy would be cast down, where people would be judged by the humility of their spirits, not the grandeur of their possessions. Again, these teachings have the potential to transform the world into a place where wealth is distributed equitably and all people are considered worthy.

I believe that my efforts to lead a life of simplicity, and the efforts of Mennonites and others around the world to do the same, have the potential to turn our world on its head. Valuing simplicity over the accumulation of wealth and possessions paves the way for a more equitable and just distribution of the world's resources. When I utilize only what I need, there is something left over for others to do the same. When I measure my own self-worth and that of others with a yardstick other than that of personal wealth, I create freedom from the pervasive pressure in our world to have more. When I am content with less than what society tells me I need, I am free from the anxiety that plagues many of my generation because of predictions of downward mobility in our society. Being a Mennonite gives me a theology and a community of support from which to pursue this lifestyle.

I am a Mennonite because Mennonites believe in the church as a prophetic witness to the world. Jesus encouraged his followers to freely "nonconform" to the expectations of society, to make the goals of his kingdom their aspirations instead. Jesus encouraged his followers to support each other and together be a witness for change that would make our world more like the kingdom of God.

I take great pride in being a part of a faith community that is recognized for its nonconformity—for its simple lifestyle, its efforts to make peace, and its efforts to speak and act for justice and equality. The Mennonite church is not perfect. There will always be gaps between individuals' or institutions' theology and practice. But I find the heritage of prophetic witness in the Mennonite church inspiring. And I find great strength in the fact that I am not merely an individual trying to bring about the kingdom of God, but that I am part of a community of faith worldwide that is attempting to do the same by creating elements of that kingdom where it can. Being a Mennonite gives me a theology and a community of support from which to transform the world.

You and I live in the same world. We are probably concerned with many of the same issues that affect our own future and the future of our generation and our world. I invite you to commit yourself to the Mennonite community of faith as one way of responding to those concerns. The Mennonite church doesn't have all the answers to all the hard questions you are asking, but it can provide you with a framework from which to approach them. Furthermore, it can provide you with a community of support and discernment as you struggle to be a faithful disciple of Christ.

As I mentioned earlier, the Mennonite church is not perfect. The tradition to which it is an heir is a radical one that can easily lose its edge in a world of significant pressure and upheaval. That is precisely why the Mennonite church needs you. The energy and idealism of young adults like yourself is essential if the Mennonite church is truly going to maintain this radical edge in theology and practice. Your questions, challenges, hurts, and ideals may be hard for the church to hear at times, but they are so important to help the church maintain its vision of a prophetic community modeling Christ's love in the world.

When Jesus calls us not to take an eye for an eye and a tooth for a tooth, the church needs you to remind it that the justice systems of our countries practice just such retributive justice. The church needs you to envision and implement creative alternatives to this sort of retaliation. When Jesus tells us that the lowly are blessed, the church needs you to remind it that even the most outcast and rejected of our society should be welcome in our churches. The church needs you to extend that welcoming hand and so encourage others to do the same. When Jesus says it is easier for a camel to go through the eye of a needle than for a wealthy person to enter heaven, the church needs you to remind it that the wealth and greed of our society pervades even our churches. The church needs you to go out on a limb and challenge the notion that we are entitled to prosperity, that it must be seen as our reward from God. The church needs you to work for change in this generation and to survive to work for change in the next generation. I invite you to accept this challenge and to become a part of a faith community that has the potential to transform the world.

 QUESTIONS FOR DISCUSSION

1. The Mennonite church, or at least certain segments of it, is often accused of being too preoccupied with Jesus' social agenda and not concerned enough with Jesus' invitation to personal salvation. Do you think this is the case? Can the two really be separated?

2. How faithfully do you feel the Mennonite church is living out its radical theology in the world? Does this encourage you to commit yourself to this community of faith, or does it discourage you from doing so?

About the Author

Pam Peters-Pries has been involved in congregational and conference-wide young adult ministry since 1990. Still in her twenties, Pam's experience includes speaking and writing a regular column on young adult themes.

She holds bachelors degrees in theology from Canadian Mennonite Bible College in Winnipeg and in philosophy from the University of Saskatchewan.

Pam grew up on a farm in Saskatchewan and has also lived in Manitoba. She and her husband Albert live on a rural acreage with their two young children.